SO-AGR-250

GIVING BACK

Discover your values
and put them into action through
volunteering and donating

Steven P. Ketchpel, PhD

Jonquil Press
Berkeley, California

Copyright © 2012 by Steven P. Ketchpel, Ph.D.

All rights reserved. No part of this book may be reproduced or utilized in any form or by any means, electronic or mechanical, including photocopying, recording, or by any information storage and retrieval system, without permission in writing from the author, except for brief passages in connection with a review.

Editor: *Nancy Carleton, NancyCarleton.com*
Cover Photographs: © *Jason Koenig, jkoephoto.com, used by permission*
Author Photograph: *Hector Garcia-Molina*
Book Composition: *Marites D. Bautista*
Design Consultant: *Dave Blake*

To order additional copies of *Giving Back*, visit www.giving-back.info/buy

Library of Congress Cataloging-in-Publication Data

Ketchpel, Steven P., 1971–
  Giving back : discover your values and put them into action through volunteering and donating / Steven P. Ketchpel.
     p. cm.
  Includes bibliographical references.
  Summary: "A guidebook to discovering the ways to help others by volunteering and donating" —Provided by publisher.
  ISBN 978-0-935079-30-2
  1. Voluntarism. 2. Charitable uses, trusts, and foundations. 3. Voluntarism—United States. 4. Charitable uses, trusts, and foundations—United States. I. Title.
  HN49.V64K48 2012
  302'.14—dc23
                        2012027050

Printed in the United States of America.

10 9 8 7 6 5 4 3 2 1

To my parents,
Pat and Paul Ketchpel,
for their teaching by example

Contents

List of Exercises & Charts

NOTE: The worksheets marked with an asterisk are also available for downloading at my website at www.giving-back.info free of charge.

List of Givers' Stories

Preface

"I'm sorry," he said. "It's hard for me to see. I'm very nearsighted."

Edward was a tall, slender man in his midthirties with a full, close-cropped beard. He was a guest at Hotel de Zink, a homeless shelter hosted that month by my church in Palo Alto, California, and I was volunteering that evening. I accepted his apology and mentioned that I, too, was very nearsighted—legally blind without my glasses.

"My vision is 20/400," Edward told me. He'd been without glasses for several months, and consequently was functionally blind. He hadn't been able to work, and even filling out job applications was difficult. I thought back to the world I'd known before getting my first pair of glasses in seventh grade: not being able to see clearly what was written on the blackboard, and not knowing when people were looking at and talking to *me* or just someone in my direction. Wearing glasses to correct my nearsightedness is a blessing I place at the top of my list, though too often take entirely for granted.

Over the years my vision had degraded and now matched Edward's 20/400 acuity (or lack thereof). "Mine, too," I said. "Twenty/four hundred." When I asked whether he knew his precise prescription measurements, he replied with details that were strikingly close to mine. "Would you like to try my glasses?" I offered.

Edward hesitated a moment—it was a rather intimate gesture, pushing hard against both of our comfort zones. Curiosity got the better of him, and he put on the glasses, marveling, as I had as a twelve-year-old, at the clarity of corrected vision after not having it for such a long time.

When I returned the next day, I had a gift for Edward: a pair of my old glasses and some sets of disposable contact lenses. While the frames were perhaps not the style Edward would have chosen, he was very grateful. It was immensely gratifying to me, almost as if I were a doctor able to restore someone's sight. But it was also humbling and a bit unnerving; the similarity of our prescriptions and our ages was a reminder of the common humanity joining us despite the difference in where we sleep. All in all, it was a tangible demonstration of how much difference a seemingly small gift can make in a person's life and the joy that giving back can bring.

My own road to volunteering and giving started early. Even before I was born, my parents were involved at their church and in Scouting, as well as more informally in spreading kindnesses around the neighborhood, so I grew up with volunteering as a regular part of my life.

In Boy Scouts, the adult troop leaders sometimes organized volunteer service projects, but more often we worked on Eagle Projects, which the older boys of the troop organized. An Eagle Project was the capstone requirement for obtaining the top rank on the advancement ladder. To fulfill it, a Life-rank Scout (just below Eagle) conceived a service project and led the efforts of others to carry it out. Over the years I participated in projects such as building a *sukkah* (outdoor hut) for the local Jewish temple, clearing hiking trails, and helping to line the main street in town with flags on Memorial Day. My own Eagle Project was an early opportunity to develop leadership in giving back, and to feel the appreciation of my church community as they benefited from computerized membership records.

During college and graduate school, my class work and research, as well as teaching assistantships and the hours spent backstage helping with theater productions, meant that I had little extra time for volunteering. After earning my degrees, I joined a startup, where I barely had time to sleep, much less volunteer. Still, I had the sense that giving back was an important part of leading a successful life, and one I'd return to when the time was right.

You might predict that my life followed the plotline from a fairy tale, and my company went public, leaving me the free time and available funds to give back on a grand scale, and write a book celebrating my success in pursuing humanitarian causes. No, my path was more prosaic. After six years of working long hours and focusing on the company's success, the company was sold at a loss, and I found myself without the job that had consumed me for years. I became involved in a volunteer technical project on microfinance (which I'll talk more about in Chapter 9) and served on the board of directors of a nonprofit, working hard to raise the funds for our executive director's modest salary. Mostly, I'd meet with prospective donors to discuss our organization's projects and learn about the other causes the person supported. During the course of these conversations, I saw firsthand how people's choices about giving back represented their greatest hopes for the future. I was impressed by their commitment, and inspired by the way they were using their resources to back up their beliefs. I resolved that, like them, I'd look for the ways that my gifts of time, talent, and treasure could have the greatest impact.

While I wasn't in a position to make huge donations, I believed I could use my technical skills in website traffic analysis to help larger organizations that relied on the Internet to publicize their message and to attract supporters. I focused on the organizations that were in a position to use my time and talents the best, and ended up working with several. This involvement cemented my understanding of the win-win-win nature of giving back:

* ❖ My efforts were helping the nonprofit organization: I could see that my contributions (both the time and the money that I was giving) were enabling them to be more successful at their mission.
* ❖ This, in turn, helped the beneficiaries: When an organization such as DonorsChoose was able to understand and serve their donors better, donors returned with more and larger gifts, funding more classroom projects. Grameen Foundation created special software and shared it with their partners to track the microcredit loans that helped women in the developing world start their own businesses.
* ❖ All the while, I was also benefiting: It was rewarding to see the difference that my efforts were making. In addition, I made many friends and developed skills that I wouldn't have otherwise. Finally, the exposure to the issues that the organizations were dealing with, and the solutions that they chose to implement, gave me a greater perspective on the social causes that I was interested in.

I was convinced and hooked: By giving back, I was helping others and helping myself. I was proud of the difference that I was making, and I felt energized knowing that people were counting on me. I learned more and had more fun.

How could I help others see this opportunity and get more involved in giving back?

I spoke with friends and encouraged several to get involved in various projects. It was rewarding to see them start to give back, but I soon realized I'd never reach many people if I were limited to one-on-one conversations. That got me thinking about alternative ways of sharing my ideas with people, and the idea of writing this book took root.

As a computer scientist, I tend to think about process: Is there a series of steps you can follow to accomplish a goal? I believe there are many people who are predisposed to give back, and even more who will be when they hear about the benefits. One of the stumbling blocks that keep people from getting involved is the lack of a clear path to do it. I hope this book will provide that path.

Thinking of my own path to giving back, I realize that getting started early was instrumental in my more recent involvement. My parents' encouragement had played a role, and my early volunteering experience made it seem less of a challenge to get involved. So I hope families with younger children will read this book, involving more young people, and building a lifetime habit and a family legacy. I also believe that the goodwill and collaborative habits generated by giving back will show up in other family interactions, benefiting everyone involved.

So, while I believe that anyone can benefit from giving back, and this book can help you get started, I'm especially excited by the prospect of inspiring families. Certain optional sections of the book are designed as family discussions, with special introductions for children participating in them.

If you follow the process outlined in *Giving Back*, you'll likely find that helping others makes your own life richer. You'll likely experience some positive side effects, such as stronger ties within your family and kids who are motivated to make a difference if you engage your family in the process, and the possibility of making new friendships and developing new skills if you're an individual. It's an exciting journey with a great destination, and I look forward to being your guide along the way.

—SPK

A Map to Using This Guidebook

Everybody can be great. Because anybody can serve. You don't have to have a college degree to serve. You don't have to make your subject and your verb agree to serve. . . . You don't have to know the second theory of thermodynamics in physics to serve. You only need a heart full of grace. A soul generated by love.

—Martin Luther King Jr.

Giving Back is a guidebook to help you discover the ways you can help others by volunteering and donating. It's not a book to read in a single sitting but rather to use as a companion over the weeks and months as you get more deeply involved in your passions. It includes exercises that will help you identify the issues that have the most meaning to you, and demonstrate how you might use your skills and time to address them. Giving back can also be an important way for a family to connect with one another and perhaps with a legacy of generosity established by previous generations. Some of the exercises in this book involve discussions with other family members, though if you're reading this book on your own, you'll also benefit from thinking about the answers.

The following *visual table of contents* shows the relationship between the topics, with the arrows indicating the order of the chapters. The chapters on the left-hand side of the figure address *volunteering*, giving your time and skills, while the chapters on the right-hand side focus on *donating*, giving your money. Aside from the box containing the four chapters about creating a strategic volunteering plan, which comprise a logical unit, your path through the rest of the chapters can be more flexible. Feel free to skip around to the topics that will be most helpful for the next steps in developing your own plan for giving back.

VISUAL TABLE OF CONTENTS

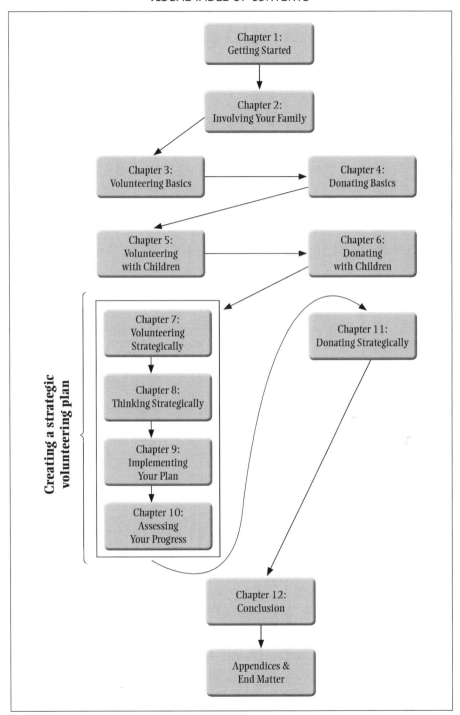

If you decide to follow the book in chronological order, here's what to expect in each chapter. Note that sprinkled throughout are givers' stories, related to the material and great sources of inspiration for your own giving, as well as exercises designed to help you make the most of the material.

Chronological Outline of Chapters

Chapter 1

A basic introduction to my views on giving, why it's important, and what you can hope to get out of this book. Some different motivations for giving and excuses for not giving, as well as how your (or your child's) understanding of giving might develop over a lifetime.

Chapter 2

A description of the benefits of involving your family, and guidelines for the Listening & Learning Conversations that you'll have during the process.

Chapter 3

Everything you need to get started with your first volunteering experience, including a series of questions to help you think about what you want to do (along with a dose of reality for what you're likely to be offered) and a list of websites to help you find possible projects, as well as tips on finding projects not listed on the Internet.

Chapter 4

Questions to help you clarify your thinking about donating money, with different guidelines to consider, such as how much you'd like to give, how to spread it around, and whether you'd prefer to give anonymously. A collection of websites to help you ensure that the places you give to will make good use of the money. Comments about two tough groups of people asking for money: relatives and panhandlers.

Chapter 5

Considerations for involving your children in volunteering projects, along with age-appropriate ideas for children from five to eighteen. Information about volunteering vacations and a *gap year* of service.

Chapter 6

Teaching children about the importance of sharing financial resources with those who have less. Ideas for encouraging giving, such as gift matching and *birthdays for charity.*

Chapter 7

Taking stock of the volunteering you currently do, with questions to help you uncover your giving passions and to get you and your family thinking about the causes that matter most to you. A prioritization exercise to help you allocate your volunteering time, and a skills/desires assessment to help you consider how to maximize the satisfaction you receive from volunteering.

Chapter 8

A library of templates you can apply to think creatively about making a significant change for the causes that are important to you.

Chapter 9

A strategy to help you find the organizations working on the causes that are important to you, and a discussion of the ways metrics can be used (and misused) to evaluate their effectiveness. A checklist of things to look for in choosing which organization to work for, or if you need to start a new nonprofit yourself.

Chapter 10

Evaluating your satisfaction with your volunteering strategy over time.

Chapter 11

A grab bag of topics related to financial gifts: matching gifts (where yours is being matched by an employer or you're doing the matching to inspire other givers); ways to maximize the tax benefits of your giving, including donor-advised funds (DAFs); giving cars or your professional services; estate planning for gifts after your death; and added options for wealthy givers.

Chapter 12

A summary, with time for reflection and celebration.

Appendix A

Some comments on reviewing a nonprofit's IRS filing, called the 990 form, to scan for potential warning signs or to provide reassurance about a nonprofit you'd like to support.

Appendix B

Tips for deciding if starting a new nonprofit is the right thing for you, along with initial steps if it is.

Appendix C

A list of the Internet resources referred to throughout the book.

End Matter

A Bibliography of related materials and the author's Acknowledgments.

Alternative Approaches to the Book

This section addresses some shortcuts for approaching the material in *Giving Back* depending on your goals.

Shortcuts for Those Eager to Get Started

Since you may want to spend more of your time volunteering than reading, feel free to jump directly to Chapter 3, Volunteering Basics. If you're planning to include your children in your volunteering experience, Chapter 2 provides a bit more introduction, and Chapter 5 is a good place to learn about age-appropriate volunteer activities. Those chapters will likely be enough to get you going, and you can come back to Chapters 7 through 10 when you're ready to commit to a larger-scale volunteering project and want to think strategically about how to do it. The sections on donating (Chapters 4, 6, and 11) will be relevant as you think about how you'd like to share your financial resources, with Chapter 11 offering more detail on the basics covered in Chapter 4.

Shortcuts for Family-Oriented Givers

One of the main themes of this book is that teaching your children about giving is an important part of raising them. If this is your main motivation for choosing this book, you'll be most interested in Chapters 2, 5, and 6, which are full of resources for introducing your children to the topics of volunteering and donating, with tips on how to get them involved not just in the activities but also in the discussions and the decision process. Giving provides the teachable moments that allow you to pass on the values of compassion, generosity, and respect for others. The family Listening & Learning Conversations introduced in Chapter 2 and offered in Chapters 7, 9, and 10 reinforce the action with reflection about why giving back is important. Chapters 7 through 10 are for the families that want to delve deeper and make volunteering a core part of their family purpose. Chapter 11 addresses donating strategically, with topics appropriate for families with older children, such as leaving a legacy.

Shortcuts for Those with More Money than Time

Perhaps you're daunted by the prospect of carving out a meaningful chunk of time to volunteer. You may be in the key stages of establishing your career, or in a demanding position at work that requires your full concentration. Maybe you've reached a stage in your life where your energy supply or physical ability is limited. These are just a few of the reasons you might consider donating your money to organizations, in essence hiring them to do the things that you can't take on yourself. Nonprofit organizations rely on gifts from donors to carry out their work. If you'd like to learn more about giving financially, Chapter 4 is a good place to start. Chapter 6 is applicable if you'd like to involve your children in the decisions about donating. Chapter 11 provides further information about strategic giving, especially applicable when you have the resources to make a larger difference to the organizations you support. Appendix A is designed to help you perform due diligence on the organizations you're considering, to make sure that your gift will be used well.

Shortcuts for Those with a Fire in the Belly

Thank you! Those who have big ambitions for their giving are the type of people who can truly make a difference in our world. You may already know what cause you wish to devote your time to, and perhaps you've already spent some time volunteering on it. In that case, Chapters 8 through 10 can help you maximize your impact, and Appendix B has some basic information to help you decide whether it makes sense to start your own nonprofit. The financial support of your cause is critical to making large-scale change, so Chapters 4 and 11 will help you think about monetary giving and can be of aid whether you're thinking of your own resources or of fundraising from other people. Chapters 5 and

6 and the Listening & Learning Conversations in Chapters 7, 9, and 10 can help you share your passion for giving with your children. If you haven't found the cause that really evokes your passion yet, Chapters 3 and 7 may provide some inspiration to get you going.

Setting Up a Giving-Back Binder or Notebook

Finally, to get the most out of *Giving Back*, I encourage you to set up a binder or notebook as you go through the chapters most relevant to you. In it, you can engage with the exercises, make notes to follow up on later, and plot your own course toward more effective giving and volunteering. To make it easier for you, I've included grids for the tabular portions of the exercises at my website, www.giving-back.info; please visit and download these grids free of charge.

CHAPTER 1

Getting Started

The secret of getting ahead is getting started.
The secret of getting started is breaking your complex overwhelming
tasks into small manageable tasks, and then starting on the first one.

—Mark Twain

Americans are a generous bunch. America's organizing principles include the protection of individual liberties and the preservation of the common good. We have a history of participating in public discourse, of collaborating to provide universal education, and of sharing the costs for building and maintaining our roads, libraries, and sewers. Our democratic government protects the rights and provides for the basic welfare of our people.

America's tradition of generosity is also a more personal affair, not relying exclusively on the government. Collectively, we give billions of dollars and billions of volunteer hours to nonprofit causes each year. We support arts and cultural events, colleges and universities, houses of worship, and medical research. We help care for animals that have been mistreated, and send food and financial aid to countries ravaged by war or natural disaster. We give money to homeless people, and we give money to help build new places for them to live. We give money to organizations that treat mental illness and substance abuse, and we give money to organizations that work to change our law and tax structure to make it more likely that the homeless will find housing. We also give time: We pound nails into those new houses going up; we answer phones on crisis hotlines; we write letters supporting legislation; we educate our friends about the causes we care about and solicit their support for the solutions we think will be effective.

By sharing what we have, the world is a better place. Giving back starts with an appreciation for what we have, recognizing that many factors outside our control were necessary for us to receive it. Interdependence, not independence, is the primary model. In a world where nearly 3 billion people live on

$2 a day or less, the United States is a nation of great wealth. I believe that our practice of mutual support makes us a stronger nation. Being willing to help a neighbor in need or donating to a community arts center is a vital part of the social contract. This giving and receiving forms the thread of our social fabric, and reminds us of our common lot. It's also a practice we're called on to renew continually, or else it risks slipping into a forgotten past displaced by self-centeredness and distrust.

The United States is a world leader in volunteerism. According to the United Nations Volunteers' report (United Nations Volunteers, 2011), the United States is fifth (behind Sweden, Norway, France, and the United Kingdom) for the percentage of Gross Domestic Product (GDP) made up by the value of volunteering. The benefit isn't just economic. The report also offers this important conclusion: "Above all, volunteerism is about the relationships that it can create and sustain among the citizens of a country."

What Is Giving Back?

While there are many ways to give back, the two most obvious are giving back money (donating) and giving back time and skills (volunteering). This book addresses both, whether you're just getting started or are making the leap to more strategic giving. Giving back is also an important lesson to teach our children, one better absorbed through action and reflection, not just hypothetically.

There's a dizzying range of options in how to give back: You can write a check to support cancer research. You can serve as a Little League coach. You can train a guide dog for the blind. You can organize a carwash to raise money for orphans in Africa. With the possibilities limited only by your imagination, it can be overwhelming to decide where to give back and how to start.

This book is designed to help you think through the ways you'd like to give back, and many of the chapters include exercises to help you go deeper. Whether or not you've devoted much time to thinking about these topics or articulating your beliefs, you make choices every day that reveal them. By working through the exercises in the giving-back notebook you set up (and utilizing the downloadable grids available at my website, www.giving-back. info), you'll come to a better understanding of what your values are, how you currently express those values, and whether and how you'd like to change the way you express them.

Giving back is about your values and how you put them into action: Your gifts of vision, time, and money will bring the world closer to your ideal.

Giving back is about putting your money where your heart is. Giving time is giving of yourself, using your skills to advance the causes you believe in. Thinking carefully about how and where you give your gifts will maximize their impact.

Giving back is about self-worth: It's about spending your limited resources of time and money in a way that's consistent with how you view yourself and how you'd like others to see you. It can strengthen your sense of self-worth and pride. Giving back and knowing the impact you're making in the world can lead to greater happiness and satisfaction.

Giving back is about maturity, coming of age, and power: Caring for those beyond your immediate family is a sign that you've succeeded in moving

Moms Start Raising Peacemakers Group

When their three children were just four years old, Dr. Somava "Soma" Stout, Dr. Farjam Mohtadi, and Marta Kuperwasser—a doctor, an educator, and a manager who were all first-time moms from different cultural backgrounds—decided they needed to find a way to help their children learn how to create peace in themselves and in the world around them. They organized a special parent-child weekly play group for their children and their children's friends. Following principles from the Baha'i Faith and designed to help children build emotional intelligence, virtues, and concrete skills in peacemaking, the weekly classes evolved into a community where parents and children could share important lessons and shape the way they interacted with their classmates, siblings, family, and community. The Raising Peacemakers program, as it was called, was very popular with both the children and adults; each year, Soma and the other leaders added more material appropriate for the children as they grew. Raising Peacemakers spread organically from Lexington, Massachusetts, to other communities in Massachusetts, then to other states, and even to other countries.

The ten Peacemaker Principles* provide the framework for a community of respect, action, and fun. By recognizing the potential of each child, participation is strong, and the groups achieve amazing results. The gratitude circle included in the Listening & Learning Conversations in this book is inspired by a weekly practice in Raising Peacemakers, where parents describe something they saw their children do to create peace in themselves or in the world during the week. Each child gives his or her own report as well.

---

*See www.RaisingPeacemakers.org.

beyond self-interest. Exerting control over resources (time and money) is a type of power. Giving back is about choosing to use that power for unselfish ends.

Giving back is about history: You may be taking the assets accumulated over a lifetime (intellectual, experiential, and financial) and determining how to pass them on. The choices you make will convey what's important to you. Your children and grandchildren may gain a greater appreciation of your values toward other people and toward money. You may be continuing a family legacy of giving or starting one.

Giving back is about the future: By investing today, you help bring about a better world—whether that means a cleaner environment, more cultural options in your city, stronger public schools, or the elimination of diseases through medical research or widespread vaccination.

Giving back is about empowering your children: Volunteering together can be a great family-bonding experience. Involving your children in the discussions and decisions about giving is a step toward their developing

Teen Partners with a Sister School in Haiti

Grace Linderholm, age seventeen, and her mother, a physician, were in Haiti after the earthquake of 2010, when they met Pastor Charles Henry, the founder and principal of the Victor Hugo School. Moved by the disparity between what she saw there and the abundance of her own school, Grace knew she had to help. "I realized there are certain moments in your life when you know you have to act. It's not a bleeding-heart moment, or pet project; it's the simple will of the human conscience. After seeing the living conditions and level of poverty in Haiti, I knew there was no walking away from that." Her response was to set up the Global Chalkboard Fund, using a sister-school model to enable children across the world to help one another learn and grow. The money and school supplies they've raised saved the Victor Hugo School's summer camp and provided essential materials for the classrooms. Grace also acknowledged One World Children's Fund for supporting the project and showing her how to champion the needs of the Haitian schoolchildren.*

"I believe that no matter who you are, and no matter what your age is, everyone has those burnings of compassion within them, is capable of making a difference. And I think that our story—an NGO created by a child, run by children, to help children—just proves that anyone can make a difference," Grace said.

---

* Story used with the permission of One World Children's Fund, www.owcf.org.

independence. Helping them find the causes they feel passionate about, and stepping back while they discover their capabilities, provides growing experiences in their emerging maturity. Along the way it can lead to stronger family ties.

The decision to give back can be motivated by many different beliefs:

❖ *Obligation:* Being well-off brings with it the responsibility to provide for those who aren't well-off; earlier help you received creates a debt you must repay.

❖ *Karma:* The sense that your treatment of others will come back to you.

❖ *Fulfillment:* The satisfaction that comes from helping others, whether it's from within yourself, from the appreciation of the people who you helped, or the recognition of a third party.

❖ *Peer pressure:* In a work setting or close-knit community, you may feel you will be criticized if you don't give at least as much as others do.

❖ *Prestige:* Attempting to distinguish yourself through the generosity of your giving.

❖ *Perks:* Some organizations offer their donors and volunteers more than recognition; it might be a thank-you gift or exclusive events for top givers.

In addition to reasons responsible for your giving as a whole, your reasons to make a specific gift might include:

❖ *Inertia:* You automatically give to a group again because you gave in the past.

❖ *Sense of obligation to the asker:* If a friend or work colleague asks you to give, you may be worried the relationship will be hurt if you decline.

❖ *Sense of obligation to the cause or organization:* If you or a family member received help from an organization, you may feel pressure to support the organization when it asks for your help in the future.

❖ *Reputation of the organization:* The organization you're supporting may be well rated by third-party agencies, have a long history working in the field, or have important people on its board of directors.

❖ *Belief in the organization's strategy:* You understand how the organization works to achieve its mission and consider it to be both effective (accomplishing what it sets out to do) and efficient (doing so without wasting resources).

Regardless of the specific motivation, ultimately giving back is about finding a way to use your resources (skills, time, money, and influence) to help others and advance the causes you believe will make the world a better place.

Of course, there are reasons people choose *not* to give as well. Have any of the following reasons held you back from giving?

- ❖ *Never thought about it:* It never occurred to you that a particular problem or cause could be improved by your giving or involvement.
- ❖ *Scarcity:* You were concerned that as a result of giving, you wouldn't have enough for yourself or your family.
- ❖ *Unclear how to give:* You wanted to make a difference, but didn't know what you could do.
- ❖ *Belief that modest amounts don't matter:* You may have felt that if you couldn't give a large gift, there was no point in making a smaller gift.
- ❖ *Money wouldn't be used well:* You were skeptical about your money being used productively, with concerns that it would be consumed in organizational overhead or fundraising.
- ❖ *Government should take care of the problem:* You believed that tax-supported government services should be sufficient to alleviate the problem, and therefore giving beyond paying taxes was unnecessary.

If you've found yourself nodding in agreement at any of the items on this list, notice that many of the objections relate to not having enough information. Reading this book will give you the tools to create a giving plan that is sustainable for your family and meaningful to those organizations addressing the causes that matter to you. Our generosity depends on a fragile equilibrium. Each generation is called on to rededicate itself to the notion that giving back is a part of creating the society in which we aspire to live.

Capacity for Giving Back

Family life is full. Between work, school, running a household, and caring for children or elderly parents, most of us don't have the time to keep up with friends or pursue the hobbies we enjoyed earlier in our lives. Just making sure our children arrive at and are picked up from their myriad activities seems to be the equivalent of a full-time job. A common reaction to taking on a new commitment is "I don't have time to give now—maybe when my kids are older." Budgets are also stretched thin, and the dollars left after paying our current bills often go either to paying down credit-card balances or adding to a retirement account that's below where financial experts say it should be. Simply put, it's hard to think about giving back because it will mean making sacrifices.

Before you settle for the simple answer, think about ways you might be able to integrate giving into your life. If there were a way to feel you were making a difference to an important cause, would you be willing to give up watching your second-favorite TV show? Are there expenses you could manage more carefully? What if your daughter found an organization that she was excited to volunteer for instead of taking a dance class? Could you devote both the time and the money saved to her new chosen cause? Do you have your own dance-class equivalent—something that you do to relax or socialize but that has become habitual rather than reenergizing? Consider the change that might come from spending the time working on a cause that truly evoked your passion, meeting other people who share that passion. Don't forget to factor in the benefit of exposing your child to volunteering early on; a time investment today is likely to pay rewards in the years ahead, as your child becomes more comfortable volunteering, giving, engaging tough problems, and being a leader. If an ongoing commitment seems too big a hurdle, could you devote a day for a one-time project?

Benefits of Giving Back

According to research, giving money away makes you happier. Recent work in positive psychology showed that when people were given a surprise windfall ($20 in the experiment cited) and the choice between spending it on themselves or giving it to someone else, they typically predicted that spending it on themselves would make them happier. They turned out to be wrong: In the study, the people who were directed to use their extra money in making a gift were happier at the end of the day than those who spent the money on themselves. So, as you consider the extra purchases you make, remember that, at the end of the day, you may well be happier if you give the money away instead.*

There are also many indications that people who volunteer are healthier and less susceptible to depression, especially retirees. A collection of research results (Corporation for National and Community Service, Office of Research and Policy Development, 2007) suggests that there's a *volunteer threshold* of about one hundred hours per year, or two hours per week, that is positively linked to long-term survival rates. In his 2011 annual summary of research on the benefits of altruism (Post, 2011) Stephen Post notes positive effects for mental and physical health, lower stress levels, better sleep, and improved

---

* http://dunn.psych.ubc.ca/files/2010/12/If-Money-Doesnt-make-you-happy.Nov-12-20101.pdf

happiness. Doctors, he says, would be wise to recommend volunteering to patients for its positive health impact.

How Do You Want to Get Started?

There are different ways to get involved in giving back. You can focus on one-shot opportunities, such as signing up for a service day here or there, or responding to requests for donations that come from friends or in the mail. This is a good way to start, and I'll be covering it in Chapters 3 and 4. As you become more experienced in your giving, however, you'll likely wonder whether you could have a bigger impact—both for the causes you're supporting and on yourself and your family as donors—by being more systematic in your research and giving back. Chapters 7 through 11 combine a strategic method with listening to your heart to create a giving plan that will energize you.

The following section outlines giving opportunities at various life stages, with the first paragraph for each age group focused on volunteering and the second on donating. Of course, individual children and adults may vary slightly, and not all aspects may apply, but this will give you some good general principles to consider as you get started, and as you contemplate involving your children.

Giving Possibilities at Different Life Stages

Up to Four Years Old

Intrepid parents can bring youngsters along to certain kid-friendly projects. Ask project coordinators first, realize you may not stay as long as planned, and have snacks and toys to appease little ones.

While it's too early to consider much in the way of donating, you could provide a few impromptu coins for your child to add to a donation basket (at this stage, they'll ideally be focusing on the jingle of the coins; don't push if they're attached to keeping the coins for themselves).

Five to Eight Years Old

Children can volunteer with parents or in group settings on certain types of projects: making greeting cards for soldiers overseas, visiting people in a nursing home, doing a walkathon, or trick-or-treat for UNICEF.

Children are aware of money by this stage, and realize that some children (maybe those in another country) are less well-off than they are. Exposing children to giving money at this age (such as at church or a Salvation Army kettle) is appropriate. Expecting them to give of their own money is still a stretch for most. The most socially aware at this age may opt to ask for donations or gifts for others instead of just for gifts for themselves.

Nine to Twelve Years Old

Preteens are ready to volunteer with parents or groups like school, church, or Scouts. The range of possible projects increases to include things such as beach cleanups, writing a letter to Congress, making sandwiches for a soup kitchen, or helping a shelter care for animals.

Donations start to make more sense at this age: giving up old toys for needy children, holding fundraisers like a lemonade stand (with parental supervision). Consider offering a match for gifts that preteens make with their own money or letting them suggest an organization to receive family donations.

Thirteen to Fifteen Years Old

Group volunteering becomes more prevalent; some schools even have public-service requirements. Young teens are able to participate in most activities, though some still require parental involvement or oversight for liability reasons. Energetic teen volunteers may have their own ideas for family projects or want to convince friends and classmates to get involved in projects with real impact. Old enough to volunteer but not for paid employment, students can help, learn valuable skills, and feel good about making a difference.

Some remarkably successful fundraisers are conceived and largely carried out by teens. Providing basic oversight and making sure that the beneficiary organization is reputable is enough for the parents. Setting guidelines on what to give but permitting the child to choose where, as well as having the child participate in family giving, will help build attention to making sound giving choices.

Sixteen to Eighteen Years Old

Greater independence (and a driver's license) often means that a parent doesn't have to be involved in teens' volunteering. School service-learning projects and bolstering a college application, as well as working together with friends, can be strong motivators to volunteer. Still, devoting family time to a volunteer project, especially one teens select, can be one of the more tolerable forms of parental involvement in teens' lives.

As peer pressure ramps up, spending for gas, clothing, concerts, and impending college bills may make it a bigger sacrifice for older teens to donate their own money. Spearheading or participating in creative fundraisers through school or clubs is an important way older students can help.

Nineteen to Twenty-Two Years Old

During the college years, public-service programs give young adults both structure to join an existing project and plenty of leadership opportunities.

Young adults with limited funds and high tuition bills can still make a financial contribution by fundraising from the community.

Twenty-Three to Twenty-Six Years Old

Volunteering can be a social outlet for recent college graduates and other young adults to meet new people and engage in their new communities. It can also be a way to network for professional opportunities or gain work experience. With fewer family responsibilities, this can be a period where more hours are available to give back.

While repaying college loans and saving for a down payment on a house may take up recent graduates' disposable income, it's a good time to make a commitment to a basic level of giving from a salary.

Twenty-Seven to Thirty-Five Years Old

Starting a family with the associated time investment of raising children often means that there will be little opportunity to do sustained volunteering. Professionally, there may be longer hours while getting established and climbing the corporate ladder.

With many competing demands for the household income, maintaining a modest set of gifts from current income is a good goal.

Thirty-Six to Fifty Years Old

This midcareer period is a good time to start thinking about how to involve your children in your volunteering projects (or encourage them to find interests of their own). Professional skills and contacts can be very valuable to nonprofits, and volunteer experience can aid personal growth as well. It's a good time to consider serving on a board or other leadership role. Support your children in their desires to give back by working with them, helping them find appropriate projects and groups, and encouraging them to share their passion with relatives and local media.

Consider devoting a portion of any increased salary from raises or promotions to causes you care about, to maintain or increase your giving percentage. This is also a good time to get involved in fundraising for your chosen cause as your network grows. Encourage your children to give by talking about the groups and causes that they're interested in, and consider offering to match gifts they make with their own money.

Fifty-One to Sixty-Five Years Old

Your additional experience and contacts make you an increasingly valuable volunteer, whether you're able to commit to an ongoing role or focus your volunteering on one-shot events. With child-raising commitments likely decreasing, you may have extra time to get involved.

College tuition bills and saving for impending retirement may decrease your ability to give financially, but maintaining giving priorities will provide a significant boost to your selected causes. Those who have built successful careers and find themselves with more resources to give can start planning and making strategic, game-changing gifts.

Sixty-Six to Eighty Years Old

The retirement years offer an exceptional opportunity to give back. The skills you've developed are applicable in the nonprofit arena, and staying involved with a cause you're passionate about can be beneficial for maintaining mental sharpness and physical health. Mentoring younger volunteers is a rewarding way to pass on your experience while helping both your protégés and the organization.

While your expenses may be lower at this time, your income has probably dropped as well. This is a good time to think about legacy gifts to organizations that you'd like to support in your will, if you haven't done so already.

Eighty-One Years Old and Beyond

There's no mandatory retirement age from volunteering, so as long as you're finding the work fulfilling, there's no reason to stop! Organizations benefit from the institutional memory that longtime volunteers bring, and the commitment itself can inspire a new generation of volunteers.

Your financial gifts over time have likely helped sustain the organizations that you care about most. This is a time for those who have been fortunate to think about what organizations could do with a more sizable gift, whether given in your lifetime or after your death.

As you can see from the opportunities for giving at each life stage, giving back can entail a combination of your time and money. It's best not to wait until the perfect opportunity presents itself; there are plenty of organizations that can benefit from whatever you have to give. It's up to you to make sure you feel there's a good fit between what you can offer and their need. Chapters 3 and 4 will outline the basics of volunteering and donating. If you're already involved, you may be able to skim these chapters and dive into the materials for resources related to giving back with children or those for more strategic givers.

CHAPTER 2

Involving Your Family

*It's not only children who grow. Parents do too. As much as we watch
to see what our children do with their lives, they are watching us
to see what we do with ours. I can't tell my children to reach
for the sun. All I can do is reach for it, myself.*

—Joyce Maynard

We all want the best for our children. We want to smooth their way
in the world and give them the tools for a happy and fulfilling life,
which we hope will include trying to make our world a better place.
Knowing we can't control the future, we still try to provide for them the best
we can. We aim to get them into the best schools and support what they're
learning in the classroom. We enroll them in extracurricular activities where
they show interest or aptitude, knowing that music lessons also build persistence, dance and gymnastics provide coordination and flexibility, and sports
programs result in better strength and stamina. Along the way, these activities may teach teamwork, creativity, and discipline, boosting self-esteem
in participants by developing expertise and offering the chance to perform
in public.

There's another set of values taught primarily through the family:
kindness, tolerance, gratitude, and service to others. While interactions
of all sorts can demonstrate these values, giving back offers a great labo-
ratory for real-world applications. By seeing their parents help others and
give thoughtfully to people in need, children absorb what it means to treat
others kindly. Interacting with people different from themselves can lead to
embracing diversity. Meeting others in different circumstances can build in
your children an appreciation for the things they have, which in turn can
foster gratitude.

Involving Your Children in Giving Back

In addition to seeing giving-back traits in action, children can learn from discussions that help teach these important life lessons. To help create your family's plan to give back, I recommend holding several structured conversations, which I call *Listening & Learning Conversations*. A *Listening & Learning Conversation* is an opportunity for each family member to share his or her view, and have the others listen carefully to what is said. It's not a debate, where people try to convince others of their own beliefs.

For this process and the conversations to work effectively, your family needs to share three qualities:

* ❖ *A desire to give back:* Until this desire is truly shared, giving back may be seen as the adults' pet project and won't generate the same sense of "We're all in this together" that can be most transformative. Building this desire as you go along is possible, but harder.
* ❖ *Existing healthy relationships with one another:* Volunteering together or sharing discussions about how to support causes will likely improve communication and respect as you see one another in a new light, but there needs to be a solid base from which to grow. Simply talking about volunteerism won't solve dysfunctional family dynamics. These are conversations and decisions that will involve listening, mutual understanding, making compromises, and offering support for tough decisions.
* ❖ *The time to give back:* Many families today are stretched very thin. They might be single-parent households, or those where one or both parents have demanding or multiple jobs. In such cases, it's hard to have the time and energy to give back on a regular basis. If this describes your family, it's still possible to be involved in giving back! You may not be able to find the time to participate in volunteering at the strategic level (Chapters 7–10), but even a one-time experience can be rewarding.

Giving back is a big topic, and requires time and space to discover and discuss. Each member of your family has his or her own beliefs about it, and deserves an opportunity to share them. This process isn't about changing people's minds. It's about listening deeply, sharing your own thoughts, looking for common ground, supporting one another where there's overlap, and respecting differences where there isn't. Ultimately, the give-and-take to make your family's giving-back plan can bring you closer together and be transformative in other areas as well.

Common Questions

"Are my kids old enough for this?"

Yes! Children of different ages have different capacities to understand and participate in giving back, and as long as you tailor your expectations and explanations to their readiness, it's possible for very young children to share in the experience of giving back. The earlier they participate, the more likely it is to be a natural part of their growing up and something they continue their whole lives. The section at the end of Chapter 1 offers a description of how different age groups might participate in giving back in time (volunteering) and money (donating), and Chapters 5 and 6 specifically address working with children.

"How will we benefit?"

Ideally, following the guidelines in this book will lead you to a level of volunteering and giving that excites you and makes you proud of the impact you're having for the causes you care about most. At the very least, if you complete the exercises in this book, you'll have a greater sense of what's important to you, deepening your self-knowledge.

If the other members of your family also participate in the age-appropriate exercises, the discussions will lead to a deeper understanding of your loved ones. You may discover surprises about what's most meaningful to them, and learn more about their goals and the type of legacy they would like to leave. You may also be surprised at the contributions from your children. As your children grow up, it's too easy to get distracted by their school schedules or boundary testing as they seek greater independence. Reflecting on these charitable topics with your children may reveal a depth of awareness and character harder to see in the day-to-day busyness of chauffeuring, laundry, homework, and meal preparation. Really listening and accepting your children's opinions in this area may lead to improved communication in other areas as well. These intergenerational conversations may also give you a greater appreciation for the choices and hopes of your own parents as they were raising you.

When you complete the discussions and planning exercises, you'll likely achieve a sense of clarity and power that comes from devoting more of your time and energy to the things that matter most. These discoveries may fundamentally change your life, perhaps even facilitating a career change so you can spend more of your time and energy on your true interests. The time may not be right for you to make a change now, and you can always revisit your plans after retirement. Maybe you'll decide that giving back needs to be deferred until after your kids are through college and tuition bills are fully paid. In any case, making a conscious choice and knowing that you've considered your options can remove nagging doubts about making better use of your time or resources.

"What if we're not the logical-process sort of people?"

My training in engineering and computer science leads me to approach problem solving by creating a structured series of steps. Some people find this a foreign way of thinking, and may feel the structure is too limiting. Others may be skeptical that a single plan could work for everyone's circumstances.

If you're one of the skeptics, please give the process a chance. There's room for flexibility within it. The general framework—which consists of proposing alternatives, seeing what you like, and changing what you don't— will probably yield a good result. At the very least, the discussions will be informative.

If you decide this still isn't the process for you, please don't give up on giving back! Many people find meaningful volunteer opportunities or nonprofit organizations they're proud to support by talking to people, reading the news, or seeing an ad online. If you're open to this sort of serendipitous discovery, don't leave it entirely to chance—keep your eyes open and ask your friends what they think about the nonprofits they're familiar with. Learn about an organization online to see if what they're doing appeals to you, and when a volunteer opportunity comes up, try it out!

Effective Listening & Learning Conversations

To get the whole family engaged in a joint project on giving back, it's important for all of you to feel involved in the research and decision process. This type of group decision process is easier with an impartial moderator facilitating the discussion, but your family can accomplish it on its own by agreeing to some ground rules.

The goal is to listen to what everyone has to say, not to try to change their opinions or offer "better" answers. Everyone needs time to speak, and if you have a tendency to speak a lot when your family is together, try to be extraconscious about holding back to let others have a chance too. The rules for a Listening & Learning Conversation are simple in concept, but not always easy to apply. To make sure that people feel like they're being heard and respected, each of the participants is asked to be an informal referee of the conversation, as in a soccer game. When the referee sees something wrong, he or she stops the action and calls out the infraction, indicating the severity with a yellow card (less severe) or a red card (more severe). While no one is kicked out of these conversations, there's still a distinction between yellow cards and red cards. Yellow cards are raised for time-based objections. If participants are taking a lot longer than their fair share of the time, or if they keep repeating the same point or making irrelevant digressions, anyone can raise a yellow card. (A sheet of construction paper torn into two-inch-wide strips makes good cards. Each person needs to have both a red and a yellow card.) Red cards are reserved for more serious violations, such as when one person is disrespectful or inconsiderate of another person. Hopefully such occurrences will be rare! Since the intent of these conversations is *listening* and *learning*, debating is also considered a red-card violation, as is trying to convince someone else to take your side. If you're carded, try not to be defensive; simply recognize the objection, apologize if you need to, and move on, doing your best to follow the spirit of the rules.

The four Listening & Learning Conversations included in Chapters 7, 9, and 10 will help you create a family giving plan. Each guided conversation follows this structure:

❖ Conversation goals
❖ General flow of conversation
❖ Special notes for parents
❖ Special notes for children
❖ Reflecting on the conversation

Special Notes for Parents

Participating in these conversations is a delicate balancing act: You want to encourage full involvement from your children, but at the same time you have a greater store of wisdom and experience to share. Since empowering your children is a key goal of this process, try holding back when you might otherwise jump in to make a point or offer an opinion. In general, it's best for a parent to start the conversation, setting a tone of respect and openness, and discuss why the conversation is important. Then, when it comes time to take turns to share individual thoughts, it's best if one of the children goes first. Otherwise, the children may squelch some of their original thoughts to conform to the structure and ideas their parents are offering.

In the same way, it's best if the children are the first to point out violations of the rules of a Listening & Learning Conversation. Standing up for oneself and identifying a reasoned defense for the perception of being treated unfairly is a growing experience. If you witness violations that would otherwise go unflagged, then it's fine for you as a parent to point them out. To the extent that you allow your children to be self-policing and respond to the complaints within the system, however, you give them an experience that will serve them well in other aspects of their lives.

Finally, remember that one of the desired outcomes of these conversations is to foster compassion and gratitude in your children. The topics of the conversations will naturally tend to develop those themes, but having their parents model compassion and gratitude during the conversations themselves will be a powerful example in practice.

Special Notes for Children

Having these talks may seem strange at first. Although it's called a *Listening & Learning Conversation*, it's very important that you do more than just listen. When it's your turn, make sure you say what you're thinking and give your answers to the questions. It's also important that you listen to what other people are saying, both your parents and siblings. By agreeing that you're old enough to take part in these talks, your parents are promising they want to hear what you have to say. You can help earn this trust by doing your part to make sure that everyone in your family gets to speak, and that when each person is speaking, everyone else is listening. If you feel that the ground rules of the Listening & Learning Conversation aren't being followed, use one of the red cards or yellow cards to stop the process, and then make sure it gets back on the right track.

There's no right or wrong answer for the questions in these discussions. They are about how you feel, what you think is important, and how you'd like the world to be. Listen to what your family members are saying, and do your best to understand what they mean. If they say something you don't understand, ask for an explanation.

Rules for Listening & Learning Conversations

1. Be present and attentive. No TV, cellphones, IM/chat for the duration.

2. Listen. The point of these conversations is to understand others' views and have them understand yours. It's not to change these views.

3. Don't interrupt. Allow the speaker to make his or her point.

4. Stick to the topic. Each of the proposed Listening & Learning Conversations has a goal. The conversation guidelines are intended to help you reach that goal in a reasonable time. If there's a more important conversation to have than the one in the outline, acknowledge that, set aside the guidelines for a future date, and have the important conversation.

5. Make sure everyone participates. These conversations are about exchanging views, and learning can't be mutual if anyone is silent or shut out.

6. Avoid talking about what someone else did or didn't do. Focus on what *you* believe and value.

7. Respect the time limit. There's a limit to the amount of time that people can pay attention, and it works best if you stick within that limit.

8. If you've stopped listening because of something the speaker is saying or doing, admit it: Raise a yellow card (for not respecting the clock) or the red card (not respecting the people). Just as a lawyer has to state his or her grounds for making an objection, justify your complaint with one of these categories:
    *   Off topic; irrelevant (clock)
    *   Repetition (clock)
    *   Droning; not respecting time limits (clock)
    *   "I need a break" (clock)
    *   Personal attack (people)
    *   Denial of someone else's reality (people)
    *   Attempting to convince or impose views (people)

9. If you've been carded, avoid an immediately defensive reaction. Even if you disagree with the reason, it won't change the reality that the other person has stopped listening. If the objection is time oriented, wrap up quickly and move on. If the objection is people oriented, take a deep breath, thank the person for being honest, make an apology if it's in order, and reframe your point.

CHAPTER 3

Volunteering Basics

You must be the change you wish to see in the world.

—Mahatma Gandhi

Giving back by spending your time and using your skills to help other people can be very rewarding. Your direct involvement gives a sense of accomplishment, and you can often meet other people who share your concerns or even meet the people you're helping.

In this chapter, you'll consider different factors to help you find a volunteering project that will be a good fit for your initial experience. The focus of this first experience is a one-time event, which is a good way to test things out. If that first experience goes well, there will be plenty of opportunities to get more involved in the ongoing operations of the group. On the other hand, you may find the first experience didn't work out in the way you expected. In that case, you can try other one-shot opportunities with different groups until you find a better fit.

As you work through this chapter, you'll be refining your ideal type of project, narrowing it down until you can find a specific group, day, and event where there's space available for you to start giving back.

Exercise: First Five Ws: Outlining Your Interests

This form, called the First Five Ws, records your interests and preferences, and helps capture the motivation that pushed you to get started giving back. The questions are the same Five Ws a news reporter asks to frame a story, though in a slightly different order: Why? Who? Where? When? What? Filling out the First Five Ws is relatively straightforward. The answers are mostly simple, factual responses, and the following form treats each question in turn. A completed example appears here (you can download a blank grid for the exercise at www.giving-back.info).

FIRST FIVE Ws: OUTLINE	
Why?	To help protect the environment
Who?	My 13 year-old daughter and I, working with a local organization
Where?	In or near Palo Alto, CA
When?	A Saturday morning in September
What?	Physical work outdoors

Going Deeper

The first question—*Why?*—may be the trickiest to answer. To spark your thinking about potential motivations, check out the following list of possible causes. It's not exhaustive, and your favorite cause may not be included. That's fine; it means that you've likely already made your choice! If none of the causes speaks to you, and you don't have another in mind, you may find the exercise in Chapter 7 more comprehensive. Also, consider activities you enjoy and already participate in, and see if there's a way to transform one of them into a giving-back project.

Possible Causes

Education and Youth

* Improving resources available
* Ensuring access for minority or nontraditional students
* Assisting those with learning challenges
* Funding or creating alternative education models (like charter schools)
* Creating educational opportunities or content outside the classroom, including mentoring
* Improving quality of teaching or administration
* Preschool programs

Social Services (U.S. or Global)

* Hunger and nutrition or food and water
* Housing
* Employment opportunities and job training

❖ Mental health
❖ Veterans
❖ Basic needs: clothing, household goods, transportation, access to health care

Arts and Culture

❖ Supporting performance by professionals
❖ Encouraging education or development within community
❖ Archiving and conserving for the future

Disaster Relief and Preparedness

❖ First response to disasters
❖ Sustained support for affected communities
❖ Preparedness and prevention for risks
❖ Creation of systems or techniques for more effective response

Medical Research and Health

❖ Vaccination or disease eradication
❖ Development of treatments and cures
❖ Providing access
❖ Public health education or programs
❖ Improving infrastructure

Environment

❖ Air quality
❖ Water quality
❖ Global warming
❖ Open space
❖ Food quality
❖ Animal (in the wild) treatment; biodiversity
❖ Animal (domesticated) treatment

Supporting Groups Facing Discrimination

❖ Race
❖ Physical or mental handicap
❖ Sexual orientation
❖ Age (senior citizens)
❖ Family status (orphans and foster children)

To answer the *Who?* question, think both about the people who'll be involved in the volunteering project, and the type of group you'd like to work with.

❖ Will other members of your family be joining you?
❖ If any are children, what are their ages?
❖ Are you planning to invite friends to join you? Are your children?
❖ Are you part of a group (like your church, Cub Scout troop, or alumni association) that's planning to volunteer together?

While it might be more fun to volunteer as part of a group, agreeing to coordinate a group project is a big undertaking, and probably shouldn't be your first volunteer experience. If you've already promised to be the liaison between your group of prospective volunteers and the nonprofit organization, it's probably better to do a dry run first by yourself or with just your family to make sure the organization is well prepared and will be able to handle your group.

Have you thought about the type of organization you'd like to work with?

❖ Informal, where you work independently, or perhaps as part of a small group of friends from your church or community
❖ Established nonprofit, where you can work within the structure they provide, benefiting from their resources and community of supporters

Mentoring Girls in Science

Zeina grew up outside the United States, in a country where volunteering was not part of the culture. When she arrived in the U.S., however, she was struck by what she saw as a discouragingly low level of expectation for girls' education in math and science. Motivated to help young girls break through this prejudice, she volunteered as a tutor and mentor with Big Brothers Big Sisters of America. Zeina chooses to focus on volunteer projects where she has a direct impact on individuals. She freely acknowledges that there are other ways of giving that help larger numbers of people, but she says the one-to-one connection generates "satisfaction that doesn't come from writing a check. I really do believe that anyone can contribute. Everyone has something to give."

Volunteering with an established nonprofit is likely to work out better for a first-time experience. While you could get a group of friends together to do a beach cleanup or visit patients at a nursing home, the experience of an established group will be smoother: They'll know what to do and have the relationships necessary, and the work will be all planned out, with the needed tools available. If it turns out to be something you want to do again, it's also easier to have the support of an organization, which may have a regular schedule of volunteer events.

Next, consider at what scale you'd like to work.

- ❖ Are you interested in focusing on your local community?
- ❖ Are there issues that appeal at a regional or state level?
- ❖ Are you more concerned with helping those in greatest need, regardless of where in the world they live?

The *Where?* and *When?* questions are probably determined by the constraints of your schedule and those of your fellow volunteers. It's wise to plan for a half-day session, or perhaps just a couple hours if you're bringing children under the age of ten. It's also good to plan to have a fun meal together after your volunteering project, giving people a chance to share their thoughts on the experience while they're still fresh in the mind.

The *What?* question relates to the type of work you'd like to do. For a one-time volunteer project, it's best to be flexible, as most organizations can't justify the training time (and the need to verify that you can be trusted to do more specialized projects competently). Realistically, your first volunteer experience is likely to be as unskilled labor. That doesn't mean that you're entirely without options, though. Perhaps some of the following responsibilities sound more enjoyable to you than others:

- ❖ Outdoor work: landscaping; beautification
- ❖ Food preparation and service
- ❖ Event facilitation: handling registration; staffing information tables
- ❖ Packing and logistics: sorting food or clothing donations; packing for distribution
- ❖ Caregiving: childcare or elder care
- ❖ Indoor work: cleaning, painting, envelope stuffing

Exercise: Second Five Ws: Detailing Your Intentions

Having completed the First Five Ws and having contemplated various potential causes and their parameters, take the next step to transform your general idea into a specific plan. The Second Five Ws takes the same basic structure, but the entries refer to the next level of detail. Here is a sample with the Second Five Ws that shows the refinement from the First Five Ws example earlier. (You can download a blank grid for the exercise at www.giving-back.info.)

SECOND FIVE Ws: DETAILS	
Why?	To help native plants thrive at a local park
Who?	My 13-year-old daughter and I, volunteering with Acterra
Where?	Pearson-Arastradero Preserve, Palo Alto, CA
When?	September 29, 2012, 9:30 AM–12:30 PM
What?	Learn about and remove invasive plant species

Finding the Right Volunteer Experience

Finding a volunteer experience that meets your desired First Five Ws can be a challenge. There are several websites offering lists of volunteer opportunities, but their coverage is spotty. If you happen to be in an area where they have critical mass, you may find hundreds of listings each month. When filtering by type of event and date, though, even the more robust lists dwindle to a handful of options. In areas of the country that are less densely populated or less wired, the online databases may not have anything close to your interest. If you persist, however, eventually you'll find the right opportunity. These sites offer some starting points.

Websites Listing Volunteer Opportunities

- ❖ All for Good (www.allforgood.org): Includes the listings from several other sites, so appears to be the most comprehensive. Offers the ability to restrict your search by geography, cause, and date range, so is a good place to start.
- ❖ VolunteerMatch (www.volunteermatch.org): Another nationwide site. The advanced search tab allows restricting the results to those opportunities

that are good for kids, teens, or groups. Although you can't easily filter the results to the date(s) you're interested in, you can sort the results by date.

❖ HandsOn Network (www.handsonnetwork.org): With 250 action centers, it lists many opportunities and has quite a bit of helpful information.

Digging Deeper for Volunteer Opportunities

If the websites just mentioned don't provide any promising leads, the search becomes trickier. Local newspapers sometimes list public-service projects, but more likely you'll need to contact potential candidate organizations and offer your services directly. GreatNonprofits.org is a website that will let you search for listings of local nonprofits by their area of action. The site also provides user reviews from past volunteers.

If online sources don't pan out, civic organizations like the Rotary Club or Lions Club may be able to refer you to groups or projects. If you're active in a church or temple, you may be able to find out about service projects there. *The Busy Family's Guide to Volunteering* (Friedman, 2003) is another great resource; it lists organizations by cause, and offers suggestions on how to get started. If you aren't able to find anything else, you can always fall back on your own initiative to organize a cleanup of the neighborhood or a nearby park, or a visit to a nursing home with crafts or games to share with the residents. The Corporation for National and Community Service runs a website called United We Serve that has toolkits (http://www.serve.org/toolkits.asp) to help you organize a group to tackle a service project such as organizing a food, clothing, or book drive or maintaining public lands.

After Your Volunteer Experience

When you finish your volunteering experience, take some time to reflect on it. First, acknowledge the success you had in trying something new, regardless of how it turned out. Think about what you enjoyed most and least about the experience. Is it a group that you'd like to work with again? How would you rate them for setting up your experience? Did you learn more about the organization and its mission? Did they describe the way your volunteering was making a difference? Did you get a chance to meet and talk with other volunteers? Did the organization do a good job of balancing the work with breaks? Were they able to accomplish what they set out to do for the day? Find out what the others who volunteered with you thought. Consider sharing your thoughts as a review on GreatNonprofits.org to help others who are looking for information.

As you get started with volunteering, it can help to experience several different groups and styles before committing to one. You don't want to promise too much to organizations and then be unable to follow through on your promises. It's better to start with modest one-time projects until you're sure you're comfortable making a longer-term commitment to the group you've chosen.

CHAPTER 4

Donating Basics

*I have observed 100,000 families over my years of investment counseling.
I always saw greater prosperity and happiness among those families
who tithed than among those who didn't.*

—Sir John Templeton, pioneer of the mutual fund

Giving money is a way of helping organizations achieve their mission. It's an investment in their capacity to implement their vision and make the world a better place. You can't possibly do everything on your own, but by hiring the groups you think will do a good job, you contribute to the overall progress. Giving money lets the organizations buy the things they need: the food and medicine to distribute to refugees, the paid staff members who will run the organization, the brochures and website informing more people

Supporting the Arts

Susan Hartzell, president of the board of directors of the San Francisco Contemporary Music Players, frets about declining support for the arts. Her family supported the cultural organizations as she was growing up. Not only did her parents attend the opera, symphony, and ballet, they were subscribers and made financial gifts as well. "Giving is so important," she said, "and being seen to give, thereby inspiring other people to give." She finds such dedication rare among today's audience. That notion of making a long-term commitment and taking responsibility for our cultural institutions seems foreign to today's givers, who are more likely, she feels, to volunteer than to contribute financially. Recognizing the important role that arts play in creating a vibrant city, San Francisco has dedicated part of the proceeds of its hotel tax to supporting culture. Government-supported arts, a model more prevalent in Europe, comes with its own dangers, though, notes Hartzell. "There are constraints. Here [in the United States] anyone can start a group and play anyone's compositions," a freedom that may change through censorship or self-censorship if arts funding becomes a political function.

about the cause, and the postage to send brochures to potential supporters. The financial support of millions of people lets organizations like the Red Cross undertake projects that are global in scale. The contributions that you make are critical to the success, even the existence, of these organizations, and your generosity makes the good work they do possible.

Ultimately, it comes down to a matter of your values and conscience, and your family's. The dollars that you give back represent a statement of what's important to you. You choose to invest those dollars in the welfare of other people and the betterment of the world rather than in things that might improve your own comfort or enjoyment. Your gift may pay dividends immediately, or the impact may be thousands of miles and even decades away. It's your money, though, and it's important you don't waste it. So, in addition to choosing the right size of the gift, it's also important to make sure you give it to someone who can make good use of it.

As you approach donating with this sense of empowerment—how your resources empower others to bring about the changes you desire—you're faced with two fundamental questions:

1. How much money will I give?
2. To whom will I give it?

How Much to Give

There's no definitive, right answer for how much should you give back. In this section, we'll consider five different approaches that suggest an appropriate range. By comparing those values, you'll get a sense for how much to give back.

1. Rule-based guidelines for giving back (such as tithing)
2. Average-based guidelines
3. Prioritizing giving back with other spending and investing
4. The implicit time-equivalent value of money
5. The subjective feel of your giving

Rule-Based Guidelines for Giving Back

Some of the earliest guidelines for giving back come from religion. Christianity, Judaism, and Islam all make financial giving a central part of the expectation for followers of the faith. Christians are asked to *tithe*, or give 10 percent of their income. Traditional Jews give *ma'aser kesafim*, also a 10 percent share. More commonly, though, Jews recognize the expectation of charity, *tzedekah*, without a specific amount or percentage being declared. The Muslim principle of *zakat* also entails a commandment to give a percentage, varying from 2.5 percent to 20 percent, of wealth (not just income, but accumulated assets) each year.

Historically, the houses of worship were the social safety net for the community, providing care for those unable to care for themselves. They were also the social centers of their community, providing a meeting place as well as the programs bringing the community together. The tithes paid the salaries of the religious leaders and others who cared for the buildings and community. Some funds were sent on to higher levels of the organization, which provided global guidance and ensured that local regions had the needed staff and resources. In short, religious institutions played many of the charitable functions associated with both nonprofits and governments today.

Tithing is an ambitious commitment. Dividing all your family's income into ten parts and giving one of them away is no small thing. With all the other demands on your family's finances, giving away 10 percent likely represents a significant sacrifice—one you will feel when you can't afford everything you'd like to buy for yourselves. Would such a generous gift put your family at risk? There are many families who do tithe, and while it may require you to stretch, Sir John Templeton's quote introducing this chapter speaks of the rewards.

One way to update the principle of tithing is to consider how the support you give to the government (through income taxes) also counts toward the commitments that were traditionally handled by church tithes. Choosing to tithe on the basis of your income after taxes is a relatively simple way to adjust for the reduction in your income. This is equivalent to assuming that about 10 percent of your tax bill goes to the types of social spending that would have been supported by churches or other nonprofits in another era.

Average-Based Guidelines for Giving Back

If the prospect of tithing seems daunting to you, you're not alone. If you look across the average percentage of income given back to charitable causes by America's households, the rate in 2011 was closer to 1.7 percent,* or about one-sixth of what the tithing practice recommends. If you're content with

---

* Calculated from 2011's $217.79 billion of individual charitable giving and $12,991 billion of personal income (see http://www.philanthropy.iupui.edu/news/2012/06/pr-GivingUSA 2012.aspx and Table 2.1, Line 1, of http://www.bea.gov/national/txt/dpga.txt respectively).

being average, take a moment to calculate what 1.7 percent of your income is (or, for a quick approximation, divide your income by sixty).

Exercise: Prioritizing Giving Back with Other Spending

The money you give back is the chunk of your income you didn't spend or invest. If we compare the category of donations against other categories of spending, does your behavior match your values? Specifically, how does your donation level compare to luxuries like vacations and entertainment? Other categories of spending aren't strictly luxuries: housing, food, transportation, medical expenses, and clothing are all examples of household expenses required to provide for your family. Look over the expenses honestly; though transportation for commuting to work or errands is a necessary expense, leasing a new high-performance car is not. If you consider the discretionary expense the amount you spend above the level required to meet the basic

DISCRETIONARY-EXPENSES CHART		
Category	**Basics**	**Discretionary/Luxury**
Entertainment	0	60 (cable) × 12 = 720 + 540 (hockey tix) = 1,260
Vacations	0	2,000 (Hawaii) + 550 (Las Vegas) = 2,550
Food	8 × 3 × 365 = 8,760 ($8/person/day × 3 people)	10,400 (restaurant & grocery spending) − 8,760 = 1,640
Housing	1,200 (2-bedroom, 1-bath apartment rent + utilities) × 12 = 14,400	1,850 (3-bedroom, 2-bath apartment rent + utilities) × 12 = 22,200 − 14,400 = 7,800
Transportation	Basic car lease + gas = $250/mo × 12 = 3,000	Luxury car lease + gas = $475/mo x 12 = $5,700 − 3,000 = 2,700
Clothing	$750 for family of 3	$1,500 − 750 = 750
Compared to		
Giving Back	0	$1,250

functional need, how much do you spend for each of these categories? A sample grid appears on p. 31. (You can download a blank grid for the exercise at www.giving-back.info.)

Luxuries and Giving Back

It's probably neither fair nor realistic to ask people to give up all their luxuries. After all, you've worked hard earning the money to treat your family and yourself to them. But as you compare the spending level of these luxuries to the amount that you give back to create a world that reflects your values, would you consider giving back at least as much as your *second* highest category of luxury spending?

A guilt-based justification isn't the only consideration. If you're fortunate enough to be saving money and making investments, you're probably intending to use the proceeds to provide for your family in the future. As you consider the causes that will make the world a better place in the future (by reducing conflict, protecting the environment, eliminating disease, and so forth), think about how the organizations addressing those problems would use the funds today. If the problems are growing at a faster rate than the interest that you're earning on your investment, it might make sense to give the money to the organizations today, so they can deploy it now, and reduce the complexity of the problems that need to be addressed in the future.

The Implicit Time-Equivalent Value of Money

"Time is money," the old expression goes; you're wise not to waste either of them! The money you earn is a mechanism for storing work you've done, so you can exchange it at a later date for things you'd like to buy. When a nonprofit organization asks you for money, they're indirectly asking for your time—the amount of time that it took you to earn that much money. If you know your hourly wage, you can simply divide the request amount by the (after-tax) hourly wage to see the demand they're making on your time. If you tend to think of your income as an annual figure, most people work about two thousand hours per year (forty hours per week in each of fifty weeks). Therefore, dividing your annual income by two thousand is a reasonable approximation to an hourly rate. Is the organization asking for an hour of your time? Five hours? Twenty hours? One hundred hours? If they had phrased their request as an ask for that amount of your time, would it have seemed reasonable? Use that guideline to determine how much stored labor in the form of cash you'd consider giving.

The Subjective Feel of Your Giving

Not all our choices can be easily described by rational choice or the self-interested pursuit of profit. Emotional factors heavily influence some decisions, and nearly all generate some emotional response such as regret, happiness, anxiety, satisfaction, or pride after the decision has been made. When you think back to your overall level of giving, and consider specific gifts you've made, what emotions come up? Are you generally happy with your decisions, or do you find yourself wishing you had taken another course of action? Notice the feelings, and then apply those findings the next time similar decisions arise, so that your past emotional experiences can help guide your future choices.

Hearing the stories of other givers can also help you anticipate how you might feel if you were to make choices similar to theirs. The website Bolder Giving (www.boldergiving.org) offers more than a hundred personal stories of people who've chosen to be exceedingly generous and give away half or more of their income or assets. These extraordinary givers describe the personal satisfaction they've received from their gifts, and the motivation they had for making them. Bolder Giving also has a free archive (registration required) of past issues of the now-defunct *More Than Money* journal, with each of the forty-three issues addressing questions donors may face as they consider their gifts.

Summing Up Your Level of Giving

Take a minute to review the different standards of giving: Are you satisfied with the percentage of your income and assets that your gifts comprise? How do your gifts compare with the other expenses that you incur during the month? Does it seem as though the gifts make up a reasonable amount of time equivalent? Is there a degree of consistency with the different approaches, and does that *feel* right? You need to understand how much you're prepared to give back before you can determine how to allocate those funds.

Allocating Your Funds for Giving Back

Givers today are flooded with requests for donations. It's hard to open your mailbox without finding an appeal from a nonprofit. The phone rings during dinner hour with an enthusiastic representative asking for your support. Organizations fill your email box with newsletters that declare how much your gift would help their mission. Neighbors stop by asking you to sponsor them in a walkathon. Online friends invite you to endorse their cause by contributing a few dollars as well as forwarding their appeal. If you live in a big city, or even a moderate-sized one, you may be accosted by panhandlers seeking your small change.

Having a plan will help you respond to these requests. Start by reviewing the gifts that you're already making. Indicate whether you made those gifts because of:

- ❖ A sense of obligation to the person making the request
- ❖ A sense of obligation to the organization
- ❖ A spur-of-the-moment response to an emotional or rational appeal
- ❖ A long-term history of giving to that group
- ❖ A belief that the gift is strategic and will make a difference in your chosen cause

Total up the gifts in each of these categories. In particular, focus on the gifts that you give from a sense of obligation to either the requester or the organization. If you assume those levels will likely be similar in the future, how much does that leave for more strategic gifts? With that number in mind, how will you divide it among the many worthy organizations that could use your help?

Twenty-Nickels Exercise

This exercise will simplify the allocation question by making it more immediately tangible, reducing the complexity as you focus on concrete things (coins or bills) rather than abstract numbers.

Needed for This Exercise

- ❖ Twenty nickels (or twenty $5 Monopoly bills)
- ❖ Five slips of paper, labeled with the five causes that are most important to you (If you aren't sure of your top five, consider skipping ahead to Chapter 7 and completing the exercises there.)

Setup

1. Place the five slips of paper with your causes on a table, each separated by several inches. Below each heading, place four nickels (twenty cents total).

Process

2. Imagine the coins represent the overall money that you have to allocate to these different causes. In the initial setup, they're divided evenly among the five different causes. Does that represent your interests? If not, move

START

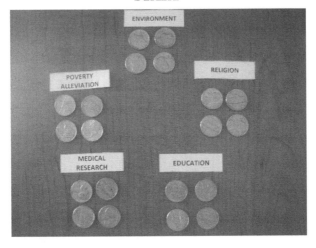

the coins around, giving additional coins to those you feel deserve more resources, taking them away from the ones that are less compelling to you. It's fine if you decide that some of the topics don't get any coins at all. If the other causes are more important, it's better to focus on them than to spread yourself too thin. Continue moving the coins around until you feel the money assigned to each cause represents its accurate importance to you.

3. When you've completed the allocation, take the total amount you have for giving, subtract out the amount you'll set aside for obligation gifts, and divide the remainder according to the allocation that you just set.

FINISH

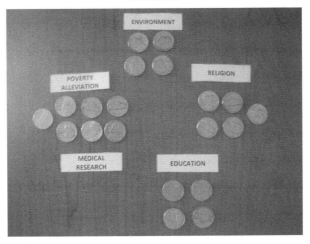

4. Once you've completed dividing your nickels, you can use an Allocation Worksheet to translate this into actual donations, making adjustments as necessary. (You can download a blank grid for this portion of the exercise at www.giving-back.info.)

ALLOCATION WORKSHEET		
Funds for donation	$2,000	
Obligation gifts	$400	
Remainder for strategic giving	$1,600	
Environment	20%	$320
Poverty alleviation	35%	$560
Religion	25%	$400
Education	20%	$320
Medical research	0%	$0

Reality Check

Realistically, with the overhead of receiving, processing, and acknowledging your donation, and soliciting you for future donations, an organization will probably spend $5 or more each year to have you on their donor list. If the percentage allocation and the available funds don't add up to a gift of at least $20, you may be better off reducing the number of gifts you're making (perhaps giving to different organizations in alternate years) and concentrating your gifts in larger amounts where they can do more.

Choosing the Organizations for Your Donations

You're probably already familiar with several organizations that deal with the causes you care about. National or local organizations have publicized themselves via word of mouth, web ads, or direct mail. Are they worthy recipients of your money? Are there others that you haven't heard of, because they're keeping their heads down and working quietly, steadily, and making a big difference?

To do your own research on an organization, their website is a good place to start.

- ❖ Does it clearly state what the organization's mission is?
- ❖ Who are they trying to help, and how?
- ❖ Does the website give some sense that they're succeeding? Is there a metric they are tracking that can show progress? Do you agree that it's a good metric?
- ❖ Are the people behind the organization (management and directors) people you trust and would like to invest in?
- ❖ Are they upfront about how much money they get each year, where it comes from, and how it's spent?
- ❖ Do they describe how new gifts will be used? Will they be used for day-to-day operations, new programs, or capital expenditures such as a new delivery truck or the purchase of environmentally sensitive marshlands?

Just as there are third-party websites that provide information about volunteer opportunities (Chapter 3), there are other sites that provide evaluations of organizations' fiscal responsibility. Mostly, these sites base their judgments on the financial forms submitted by the nonprofits to the IRS (even though they're tax-exempt, organizations need to file a 990 form each year, with the exception of churches). The sites listed in the following section allow searching by both cause and geography, as well as by name of the organization, so you can find highly rated organizations that might have a lower public profile than those with the biggest marketing budgets.

Websites Evaluating Nonprofits

- ❖ GreatNonprofits (www.GreatNonprofits.org): Compiles reviews from volunteers and donors about the organization. In addition to a star rating system, they gather the strengths and opportunities for improvement.
- ❖ Charity Navigator (www.charitynavigator.org): Focuses on more thorough analysis of larger organizations. In addition to the financial metrics from the 990 forms, a second dimension of "transparency and accountability" is measured with objective factors, such as the posting of a privacy policy. A star rating system tracks the organizational effectiveness and efficiency. GreatNonprofits' reviews of the organizations are available here as well, along with user comments. They have indicated future plans to evaluate the impact of organizations.

- GuideStar (www.guidestar.com) offers free access to recent 990 forms and GreatNonprofits' user reviews. Philanthropedia is a subsidiary of GuideStar (www.myphilanthropedia.org) that has consulted experts to evaluate the most promising nonprofits in about twenty different program areas. Although the organization coverage is limited (about four hundred organizations), they are the best as selected and reviewed by more than two thousand experts from the field. Each organization has a brief summary of the results achieved as well as a one-sentence summary of strengths and weaknesses from about twenty experts, categorized into higher-level themes.

- The Better Business Bureau (www.give.org) conducts a free evaluation of applications made by nonprofits. Those that pass a series of twenty standards of charity accountability are awarded a seal. You may file a complaint about a charity on this site.

- GiveWell (www.givewell.org) does its own thorough evaluation of the impact of organization's programs (as presented by the organization) as well as the finances. It recommends only 2 percent of the organizations considered.

- American Institute of Philanthropy (www.charitywatch.org) rates about five hundred organizations by the percentage of funds that goes to program expenses and the fundraising cost to bring in public donations, among other criteria.

- Wiser (www.wiser.org) is a network of people and organizations with a sustainability focus. Users can submit comments about organizations. WiserGiving.org is a companion site that offers a quiz to determine your giving style, and will be releasing more features to help individuals with their giving strategy.

If your organization has a BBB accreditation or a four-star ranking from CharityNavigator, you can be confident that your gift is going to a reputable organization. Smaller local organizations or religious organizations that don't fill out a 990 form are harder to evaluate. So if you don't have personal knowledge of the organization or its people, it's wise to engage cautiously before making a large gift or commitment.

By using these ratings to supplement what you found on the organizations' own sites, you'll be well informed to make your allocation decisions. Referring back to your allocation from the Twenty-Nickels Exercise, decide how you'll divide the funds among organizations within each cause. You can do another round of the Twenty-Nickels Exercise, this time choosing among organizations rather than causes, but it's fine (and probably more effective, unless you have a lot to give) to give the full amount to the best organization within each cause. You're probably wise not to split your donation if you're sending less than $20 per organization, unless you're getting on their list to receive annual reports with the intent of giving more in future years. This giving plan, which shows all your planned gifts for the year, is a powerful document because it tells you that anything that's *not* on the list (and isn't an obligation gift) will not be receiving support this year.

Cutting Off an Organization You've Given to in the Past

For organizations that you've supported for several years but that aren't part of your giving plan going forward, consider the impact of the loss on the organization. If your donation is a significant part of their budget (say, 1 percent or more of their annual funding, or, as a quick rule of thumb, $600 times the number of paid staff members), you may want to do the courtesy of letting them know you'll be reducing their support, so they have time to find alternative sources to fund their budget or to reduce their planned spending if they can't. If your gift is critical to them and you consider them a good organization, you may want to assist them by making your reallocation over two years: that is, give half of your gift to the old organization and half to the new in the first year, before transitioning entirely to the new organization in the second year. This gradual step-down will give the old organization more time to replace your gift from other sources. Of course, if you feel they aren't using your money well, you're under no obligation to give them any more.

Responding to Requests

The most important function of your giving plan is the power to say no. Once you've thought about your allocations and something comes up that's outside of your plan, the clear response is no. If the organization or individual making the request is one that neither feeds a sense of obligation nor meets your strategic vision, a simple no is all that is needed. You can soften the rejection by sharing the outlines of what you do support, and by acknowledging the value of the requester's cause or your perception of the good work that the organization is doing (if that's true), but if they're outside your giving priorities, it's better to be clear with them and potentially save both you and them time and money by asking to be removed from their solicitation list.

39

Organizations New to You

If the request is coming from an organization that's new to you but within the areas of your giving priorities, try to quickly evaluate them to see if they're worthy of your time for future giving. Can they articulate their strategy and give examples of projects they have completed? Are they knowledgeable and passionate about the topic and able to communicate their knowledge and passion clearly? Can they say how they're different from other organizations in the area (potentially those you already support)? Regardless of how compelling the pitch is, if you don't already know of the organization or the person asking for money (and consider them a part of your obligation giving), it's wisest not to give immediately. Instead, proceed with your giving plan, and consider them for next year. Doing a basic level of review, as well as not giving to an unknown person on the first call, will go a long way to protecting you against scams and fraudulent requests.

Panhandling

Having people on the street approach and ask you for money can raise a complex set of emotions. Your desire to help can be outweighed by concerns about physical safety or whether the money will be spent appropriately, and fear that giving to one individual will be unfair or result in an unmanageable number of requests from others, along with resentment at the disturbance of your daily life, and even an unpleasant reminder of the inequality and tough circumstances people face in our society. You may feel even more conflicted in some foreign countries, where the asker is more likely to be a child or suffer a physical disability or deformity, yet also could be working for or enslaved by a criminal organization that's the ultimate beneficiary of your gift. In the most egregious cases, the handlers caused the injuries to evoke pity and greater generosity.

Given the challenges, my general policy is not to give money to panhandlers. Although I'm often moved by their plight, my typical response is to look at them, offer a smile, and say, "I'm sorry, I can't help you today." I try to balance the nonresponse at the individual level with support for community organizations that provide services such as meals and housing for the unhoused and hungry people in my community. If I can easily help by directly giving food, like leftovers from a restaurant meal or a piece of fruit I happen to be carrying, I'll ask if they would like it and offer to share. I do find that acknowledging panhandlers as human beings and treating them with respect is something that I can do in most circumstances, and it's a valued response. I've had people to whom I haven't given money thank me sincerely for affirming their humanity and worth. Panhandling is a tough way to survive, and treating panhandlers with dignity and politeness can make it a little easier.

I also admire the work the Grameen Bank of Bangladesh has done with *beggar loans*. Muhammad Yunus, the founder of the bank and a Nobel Peace Prize winner for his role in developing microcredit, described the program the loan officers of Grameen Bank implemented in identifying beggars who, with

Dissenting Opinion: Giving to Panhandlers

This is one area where my heart wouldn't let my rational mind dominate the discussion entirely. Giving to someone in need in your own neighborhood is perhaps the most direct experience of donating: The person is there, asking for help, and you're there, providing it. There's no intermediary organization, no overhead, no tax deduction, no annual report—just a human response to a human need. There's also often a human story: How did it come to pass that this person's prospect of earning the money for a meal is so hopeless?

Although I don't do it frequently, making a gift to a panhandler can be an opening step in the conversation that reveals his or her story. Those stories may share common challenges and troubles, and often include illness, accidents, or addiction. Broken family relationships feature prominently. Underneath the poor outcomes and questionable decisions, however, is a human story rooted in hope, and a person clinging to that hope in spite of the hardships experienced. These conversations can remind us of our common humanity, and the need to appreciate the circumstances in which we find ourselves. I've spoken with ordained ministers, painters, and database administrators who have found themselves accepting charity for a place to stay and food to eat.

Paul Lamb, social entrepreneur and nonprofit consultant from Vallejo, California, describes his family's practice of a "giving drive-by" during the holiday season. Each person is given $20 to make a direct gift. "The point of the exercise," he says, "in addition to putting the season of giving to practice, is to experience looking into someone's eyes when you give and to give in your own community." Jon Carroll, a columnist for the *San Francisco Chronicle*, writes an annual column calling this giving the "Untied Way." He suggests giving $20 to each person who asks for money, and doing so with 1/500 of your gross annual income. A recipient's choice of how to use the money, or even lack of gratitude, isn't at issue: It's about the need and your ability to fulfill it.

an initial loan and a little support, could make the leap to being entrepreneurial door-to-door salespeople, providing a service to the community and receiving payment for it.[*]

Financial Support for Family Members in Need

"Charity begins at home." You may have heard this saying, perhaps even from a member of your extended family who needed money to make it through a tough time. It's human nature to want your relatives to have what they need to get by or, better still, to thrive. There are times when each of us needs extra support, whether that is encouragement, advice, or money. On the other hand, adding a financial obligation or expectation among family members can be the source of hard feelings and broken relationships.

Before answering a relative's request for money, think through the possible scenarios and make sure you're comfortable with the risks and are clear about your expectations.

❖ Is the money a gift or a loan you expect to be repaid? Are the expected terms of repayment (interest rate, frequency, amount) clear?

❖ Is it a one-time event, or are you prepared to provide ongoing support? If ongoing, what's the limit?

❖ Who in the family will know and who won't?

❖ Is money the best way to help? (Or would help with a job search, with applying for programs such as Medicare, or with a referral to a counseling program be more effective ways to help?)

❖ Does the person have a plan for getting reestablished?

❖ If the money is "wasted" in your view or not repaid, are you prepared for the relationship to bear the consequences?

Caring for your family's needs is a noble concern; doing so in a way that doesn't breed resentment can be tricky. Consideration and communication can reduce the risk that monetary issues will poison family ties. If you want to create a clear expectation, there are online services such as LoanBack.com or publications from Nolo Press[†] to help you clearly specify the terms of a personal loan.

---

[*] Muhammad Yunus, speech at the Commonwealth Club of California, San Francisco, January 17, 2008.

[†] http://www.nolo.com/legal-encyclopedia/promissory-notes-personal-loans-family-30118.html

Giving Anonymously

Many organizations publicly thank their donors, publishing a list of their supporters, often mentioning a level of the gift (such as $50 to $99) in an annual report or newsletter. This public statement gives some donors pause—they may prefer not to have their generosity recognized in quite so public a fashion. You do need to disclose your identity to the organization to receive the credit to deduct your gift for income tax purposes.[*] Most organizations will, however, honor your request not to mention your name related to the gift. What are the pros and cons of giving anonymously versus receiving recognition for your gift?

Pros of Giving with Your Name

1. *Appropriately receive credit for a good deed:* Giving people the chance to offer their appreciation for something you're doing is a healthy dynamic for both the giver and the recipient of the gratitude.
2. *Provide a role model for prospective givers:* By associating your name with the gift and organization, you stand behind it in a way that lets other prospective supporters see the social proof of real donors like themselves. If people who know you have questions about the organization or how past gifts were used, they might contact you to answer those questions. Think about your children among this group: Seeing your family name in a list of givers may help them think about themselves as activists involved in important causes.

Cons of Giving with Your Name

1. *Solicitations from other organizations:* Organizations sometimes share their donor lists with other groups that have common values and potentially related programs. When donor lists are made public, you can't control who finds your name and associated gift level, so you may receive solicitations from other organizations where the values match is less clear. Moreover, the list will be available to salespeople who might data mine it to find prospects for their financial management, real estate, or legal services.
2. *Connection with sensitive causes:* There may be times and particular causes where involvement may subject your family to scrutiny you'd prefer to avoid. You have the right to privacy about your giving, and if you feel that

---

[*] See Chapter 11 on donor-advised funds as a way to achieve true anonymity.

giving incognito would protect you from negative consequences, you may want to give anonymously.

3. *Different treatment:* If you've made a large gift, people within the organization (or others who see your gift) may treat you differently, either trying to butter you up for another gift or overdoing thanks for the previous one.

Giving using your own name is a second gift to the organization—it allows your reputation to provide a *halo effect* to them. You act as a leader in the community, modeling giving behavior to others, and implicitly agree to act as a reference for others with questions about the organization. It does come with a cost, though, and you need to be prepared to receive more solicitations from people who learn of your gift. If you have a well-defined giving plan, however, you'll soon learn to feel secure in your strategy to eliminate quickly requests that don't fit into it.

Giving Time vs. Giving Money

Earlier in this chapter, I noted the relationship between a request for money and the implicit time request. The flip side of this question is if it makes sense to volunteer your time, or whether the organization would be better off having the money you could earn if you were working instead of volunteering.

There are plenty of reasons volunteering can make sense, even if you have a job where an extra hour of work yields a corresponding increase in your take-home pay. One reason is you want to be a part of the organization, to work with the people on a regular basis, and to see how your direct involvement makes a difference. A related reason is if you'd like to involve other members of your family in working with an organization. Working together can be very meaningful, and may even be required if your children are young enough to need parental supervision.

You may have particular skills that are very valuable to the organization that they can't simply buy with the money you'd give. Bookkeeping skills, marketing skills (especially website development or social media), volunteer coordination, fundraising, and strategic planning are all areas where most non-profits would be very happy to have extra help. If you're able to provide those skills, try asking whether there's a way for your selected nonprofit to make use of them. (The website catchafire.org lists organizations looking for people with these professional skills to work on particular projects. It's expanding from its New York base, and you may find projects you can do entirely online.) You

Raising a Quarter Million Dollars

Vicki is an active volunteer fundraiser for the causes she supports. She talks about the different activities that she has participated in for a host of programs: coordinating a silent auction, selling raffle tickets, parking cars during events, selling scrip, making baked potatoes—and the list goes on. I ask her how much she has helped to raise, and she stops short. "It must be more than $100,000," she replies. I can tell that she has vastly underestimated, and we go back through the list of programs. Taking the low end of her estimate for each, the total quickly surpasses $250,000. It's the satisfaction of seeing the numbers, as well as the impact that the extra funds have had, that keep Vicki energized. Speaking of extras in the classrooms, like a Pico overhead projector, she said, "You know, if there weren't people out there fundraising, the schools wouldn't have it, because it's not coming from the state." She likes to be able to link the fundraiser with the benefit it provides. Vicki talked about a silent auction that netted her local school $8,000. Some of the money was set aside for an after-school homework club for the kids who need extra help. Although grant funding pays the bulk of the expense, it's not available at the start of the school year. Using the money from the auction, "the club can start the second or third week of school instead of waiting until October or November, when the grant money comes in. So it can be of more use to the kids," Vicki says.

may find that your unique skills will make a disproportionately large impact compared to the effect your money would have. On the other hand, volunteering can also be a great way to build new skills. You may be able to find a mentor within the organization who can teach you, and the context of working on a real-world project can provide better experience than a classroom setting. Finally, you may simply find the change of pace of working in a new environment on different problems preferable to the prospect of working extra hours in your regular job. Of course, the ultimate decision is yours: Choose the option that provides the greater sense of fulfillment. Just be aware that the skills you offer may be an even greater gift to both the organization and yourself than giving an equivalent amount of money.

CHAPTER 5

Volunteering with Children

Giving kids clothes and food is one thing, but it's much more important to teach them that other people besides themselves are important, and that the best thing they can do with their lives is to use them in the service of other people.

—Dolores Huerta, cofounder, United Farm Workers of America

S haring doesn't always come naturally to kids. Under the guidance of parents, they learn to take turns—letting a sibling or playmate use a coveted toy first, for example, with the promise they will get their turn next. Meltdowns are averted, and harmony ensues. A series of experiments (Fehr, Bernhard & Rockenbach, 2008)[*] let children choose how to divide small amounts of candy with another child. Willingness to share increased with age, with almost half of the seven-year-olds and eight-year-olds sharing equally (one candy each) rather than selfishly keeping both. Even young children are willing to sacrifice to help others.

The Benefits of Volunteering

Giving back is a form of sharing that may seem one-sided and unfair to a child. The first time a child learns about giving back may be in the context of giving up toys they have outgrown, sharing them with other children who don't have as many. Most children will hang on, even playing with a forgotten toy for the first time in months, asserting that the toy is still something they use and need. Parents use these teachable moments to explain the importance of treating other people fairly, or going beyond fairness to generosity, where you

---

[*] As reported by Ed Yong in http://scienceblogs.com/notrocketscience/2008/08/children_ learn_to_share_by_age_78.php.

choose to enrich others, even at a cost to yourself. The explanations are at times hard to understand, especially before the ability to empathize develops, at age five to eight.*

Volunteering allows parents to create more learning opportunities to discuss and practice compassion and generosity. It's important to talk with your children about why you're spending your time helping other people. Following through to complete the volunteer project is also important. Don't forget to ask questions as well as share your own views. Ask your children how they think their lives would be different if they were growing up in Africa, for example, or how they would feel if there weren't enough money in the household to buy any birthday gifts. Tailor the questions and discussion to the types of volunteer projects you'll be doing, and recognize that even thinking about some of these topics can be upsetting for younger children.

Books can also help give children perspective on the differences between their own circumstances and those of children and families around the world. For children eight to twelve years old, *If the World Were a Village* (Smith, 2011) makes the global statistics more manageable by interpreting them on a personal level. For younger children, books like *What the World Eats* (Menzel & D'Aluisio, 2008) and *Houses and Homes* (Morris & Heyman, 1992) offer compelling pictures of the food and shelter children have in other countries.

In addition to the altruistic benefits that come from volunteering with your children, there are a host of other benefits. Depending on the project, your children might learn a particular skill like painting or gardening. Nearly all volunteering projects involve teamwork, as everyone pitches in to accomplish the goals for the day. A project may exercise your patience, and, on occasions, your skill in getting along with difficult people. The satisfaction from a job well done is something you can enjoy with your family, and the opportunity to work together may well result in memories for years to come.

Many organizations aren't equipped to handle unaccompanied minors as volunteers. Some can't take volunteers under the age of thirteen, even when joined by a parent. Make sure you know an organization's policy before you bring your children along. Although the policies of different organizations vary, some types of volunteering are a better fit for younger children, while other volunteer opportunities are best saved for adults or teens, who might be stronger, more aware of how to relate to people (and risky situations), or

---

* Kutner, L. (2007). "How Children Develop Empathy." Psych Central. Retrieved on July 22, 2011, from http://psychcentral.com/lib/2007/how-children-develop-empathy/.

better able to maintain a longer attention span, along with possessing the self-motivation to follow instructions and finish assignments.

As children get older, you might consider taking a *volunteer vacation*, where you devote a week of service as a family, often in a part of the country or world you wouldn't otherwise visit. Upon graduating from high school a student might choose to spend a *gap year* in service rather than enrolling in college right away. The experience can be a formative one that motivates both the direction and seriousness of subsequent college studies. These longer-term volunteering options are described in following sections.

Types of Volunteer Projects Suitable for Various Age Groups

The next section describes projects suitable for various age groups. Use these as a general guideline; individual children may be more or less mature.

Suitable for Younger Children (Up to Ten)

Younger children can often bring enthusiasm to a project. They may not have the physical strength or coordination, long attention span, or attention to detail required for some projects, and of course they shouldn't be involved in projects involving physical risk or unsupervised contact with outsiders. Parental involvement is practically a must, though some school, church, or Scouting groups may be able to share the supervisory responsibility.

- ❖ *Arts and crafts projects:* Making greeting cards or holiday decorations for people who might otherwise be forgotten (soldiers or people in nursing homes or hospitals). Involving others in the crafting process can be part of the volunteer service as well.
- ❖ *Environmental:* Under the watchful eye of a parent, adult leader, or older youth, children can participate in picking up trash, cleaning up beaches, planting seedlings, and removing invasive plants.
- ❖ *Senior citizens:* Visiting senior citizens in a nursing home or their own homes can be mutually beneficial for both elders and children. Game playing, reading together, or helping out with simple household tasks are things younger children can do to provide stimulation, conversation, and practical assistance for seniors who might otherwise be isolated.
- ❖ *Hospitalized children:* A visit from a new friend of the same age can be a great way to cheer up a patient.

❖ *Food closets:* Children with adult supervision can help sort, bag, and box food donations for distribution.

❖ *Fundraising:* Walkathons, lemonade stands, coin drives, can drives, or car washes. As concerns about children going door-to-door have increased, fundraising efforts that involve neighborhood pledge or gift solicitations, or cookie, popcorn, or magazine subscription sales, have declined. Still, parents can be involved in the solicitations while the children participate in walking or selling lemonade, or encouraging relatives to share canned food.

Suitable for Tweens (Ten to Twelve)

A greater sense of independence and the ability to focus on a task at hand are two qualities that make tweens more capable volunteers than their younger siblings. They can be given more autonomy and can work independently (at home or school) on some projects. Parents can provide guidance to help tweens think through general approaches and plans, as well as be near at hand to help when children run into a problem. Encouragement and praise help sustain the effort within a single volunteering effort or across multiple days or projects. Jewish girls turning twelve might be looking for *mitzvah* projects as they prepare for their *bat mitzvah*, for example.

❖ *Nature and outdoors:* In addition to basic cleanup, children at this age can participate in doing yard work for elderly neighbors, counting birds or wildlife for scientific research, or growing food in a garden to share.

❖ *Providing childcare:* Responsible children, especially those with younger siblings, can help entertain or care for younger children at community events, assisting an adult by engaging a preschooler in creative play.

❖ *Spreading the word:* Artistic tweens might make posters or digital slideshows about a topic of interest to raise awareness and convince others to take action.

❖ *Cooking a meal or helping serve food:* Providing a meal can either be done informally for a neighbor who recently had a baby, for example, or more formally as part of a soup kitchen.

Suitable for Early Teens (Thirteen to Fifteen)

In addition to the types of activities mentioned for tweens, early teens may have the maturity to tackle bigger projects or take on leadership roles. They're also likely to prefer to volunteer with friends rather than with parents, but if there's an established pattern of working as a family on a jointly chosen

Building Libraries in Africa

When Tatiana Grossman, twelve, was preparing to take on adult responsibilities at her synagogue, she set out to enter the adult world of service too. Tati, who loved reading more than anything, learned that three out of four children in sub-Saharan Africa had no books to read. She knew exactly what she had to do. A cold call to a group that matches African schools with donors was all Tati needed to get started collecting one thousand children's books so Botswana's Sebako Primary School could have its first library. Tati's heartfelt determination, her very generous community, and a small donation table she staffed, strategically placed in front of her town's children's library, turned out to be the perfect combination. By the tenth day, Tati had collected enough books to start not one but three new libraries in Africa.

Soon after that, Tati took her private efforts public, inspiring others to follow her lead. She started Spread the Words (www.SpreadtheWords.us), a nonprofit that helps others create, support, and connect with libraries in Africa. At last count, their combined efforts have brought over twenty thousand books to five African countries, which, to Tati's surprise and her classmates' delight, earned her a finalist spot for the International Children's Peace Prize, the first ever awarded to a child from the United States.

Tati's parents note with pride the way her volunteer work has shaped the young woman she has become. Tati's impact on children in Africa has been transformative too, giving twenty-six thousand children who never had a book before the chance to love reading as much as she does.

project, especially a long-term one, volunteering can still be a family experience. Jewish boys turning thirteen might be looking for *mitzvah* projects as they prepare for their *bar mitzvah*, for example. Some middle and high schools have service requirements for their students.

DoSomething.org (www.dosomething.org) is a website designed for teens who want to take the initiative to launch their own projects. There are project ideas, videos, and tips on starting your own service club. Clubs and projects are even eligible for grants ("pizza money for your first meeting" or $500 seed grants, one awarded per week).

❖ *Office work:* Sending out donation acknowledgments, filing expense reports, or creating flyers to announce a service day can build up experience in a professional setting, add some computer or office skills, and gain the respect of the adult leaders of an organization.

❖ *Animal care:* Because of the uncertain temperament of rescue animals, shelters typically impose a fairly high age requirement on their volunteers. Early teens may be able to help with some animal related activities, but may also get stuck with barn duty—cleaning out cages and stalls.

❖ *Building and landscaping projects:* Working on home construction or remodeling projects, including repairs for seniors or upgrades to support aging in place, can give kids the chance to use tools and build skills that are fun and valuable when they have their own dorm room or apartment. Repainting a nursery school, especially by adding a colorful mural to a wall, can be both creative and fun. Planting trees or flowers can create a sense of long-term impact.

❖ *Running activities for younger children or seniors:* Teens can use their energy and creative skills to entertain others by painting faces at a community festival, putting on a show at a nursing home, or caroling at a hospital. They can also tutor others, including providing literacy training for English as a Second Language (ESL) learners.

❖ *Speaking out on issues:* Teens with a passion for social action may have time to research topics of local or global importance, summarize their findings, and write letters to the editor or participate in an essay contest. They can gather signatures for a petition and meet with government officials.

Suitable for Later Teens (Sixteen and Older)

Older teens are ready for the responsibility of working on their own with an organization or project. The work teens do with nonprofit projects can be a good preview of living and working independently of their parents. This type of experience is a great addition to a college or job application. Parents might take a more hands-off role, acting as a sounding board and providing experience when asked. If parents offer to help out with the least desirable aspects of the project—the ones hardest to fill with volunteers from among their friends (the early morning check-in for walkathon walkers, perhaps)—they will likely be accepted. Boy Scouts seeking Eagle Projects typically start working on them at age sixteen. Some high schools have service requirements for their students. DoSomething.org has more ideas for teens (see additional information on p. 50 in the Suitable for Early Teens section).

❖ *Delivering meals or medicines to shut-ins:* With the freedom of a driver's license, teens can give back by helping others who aren't able to drive anymore.

❖ *Organizing projects:* Teens can build leadership skills by coming up with their own project ideas, working with an organization to plan the details of a successful volunteer opportunity, convincing friends to participate, and inviting media to cover a feel-good story to bring even more awareness and potential donors and volunteers to their chosen cause.

Volunteering Vacations

Typically, volunteering is something you do in your own community, and you find the time to work it in around the other commitments in your family's life. If you're able to take a bigger chunk of time out to focus on a volunteer experience, it can be a memorable and very fulfilling experience. One possibility is

Chaperoning the Dance at the Senior Center

Chloé Blanchard, a seventeen-year-old from Palo Alto, California, learned to challenge her expectations about people during one of her volunteer projects. She tells the story best in her own words:

"Most of my community service ventures involve me digging up invasive plants beside Half Moon Bay, or doling out portions of soup and warm bread. This year was different. I stood at the Jewish Community Center, right beside the doors, peering inside. It was a chilly December morning, but inside the building voices burbled up and splashed over the cold with a warm, toasty feeling.

"It was to be a New Year's Eve Party. The party guests were all senior citizens, and this was to be their version of a holiday bash. In the front of the room, a band of lively old men sang an endless stream of peppy, upbeat tunes, while the guests sat and dined around beautifully decorated tables.

"I'd never thought that senior citizens could be very lively, and the possibility that they could enjoy themselves at a holiday party was the last thing in my mind. However, as I passed out food and drink, the guests spoke to me, laughing, joking, and wonderfully witty in their old age. When the dancing started, I couldn't believe my eyes. Whirling and whooshing across the dance floor, the couples twirled joyously to the music for hours, enjoying every moment.

"There's a reason why that day has become a permanent fixture in my mind, whether it was the joy and merriment experienced by all, or the stunning vitality in every senior citizen present. Either way, I'm glad to have helped these senior citizens enjoy the New Year's they deserved."

to take a *volunteering vacation*, where your family devotes a week (or more, for most international programs) to serving others. There are many organizations that offer such *mission trips* and take care of making the arrangements for you. Relying on their experience is a good way to go, unless you have a very specific project in mind and are willing to do extra legwork to handle the coordination, food, housing, and local transportation arrangements. Unless you have previous ties to a project and a specific invitation to come, showing up on your own is unlikely to lead to a rewarding experience.

The first steps in planning your volunteering vacation are determining the amount of time you have available, the type of work you'd like to do, and what part of the country or world you'd like to visit. The ages of children participating in the trip will also affect your options. With this basic information in hand, there are several websites listing organizations that offer trips:

* Volunteer Guide (www.volunteerguide.org) does a nice job of offering a selection of different organizations within each cause and approach.
* Abroad Reviews (www.abroadreviews.com) offers reviews from past travelers. They have dozens of candid reviews for the most prominent organizations, some of which warn you away from particular trips because of issues of safety, organization, or inflated cost.
* The International Volunteer Programs Association (www.Volunteer International.org) is a portal site permitting search by region, country, cause, and duration.

There are also books dedicated to volunteer vacations, and given the expense and prospect of a miserable (or unsafe!) week or two, checking out one or more is a good investment. Highly rated guides include:

* *Frommer's 500 Places Where You Can Make a Difference* by Andrew Mersmann (2009).
* *Volunteer Vacations: Short-Term Adventures That Will Benefit You and Others* by Bill McMillon and Doug Cutchins (2009, 10th edition).
* *Mapping Your Volunteer Vacation: A Workbook* by Jane Stanfield (2009).
* *The 100 Best Volunteer Vacations to Enrich Your Life* by Pam Grout (2009).

Going as part of a team from your religious group or local service organization can add to the excitement. Plus, when you return you have a built-in base of collaborators if you decide to continue your involvement through fundraising or awareness building, as many international volunteers do.

Gap-Year Volunteering

The Peace Corps (www.peacecorps.gov) is the archetype of the life-changing volunteer program. Corps volunteers take twenty-seven months to work in another country, gaining experience with the culture and sharing their skills in teaching, agriculture, information technology, or health. Idealistic recent college graduates are the most common Peace Corps volunteers, but any U.S. citizen with a bachelor's degree or three to five years of work experience may apply. The AmeriCorps program (www.americorps.gov) was launched to provide a similar experience, but for people who preferred to do their work domestically (and for ten to twelve months). The success of these programs, especially as measured by the impact on the volunteers, is substantial. Many Peace Corps alumni speak of their experience as the most meaningful period of their lives. College graduation is often a convenient time to make an extended commitment, before starting a family, buying a home, or becoming deeply involved in working in your chosen field.

Gap Years Used to Write Book, Help Microfinance

Speaking from personal experience, I heartily endorse the gap-year concept. I took my first sabbatical as I was leaving behind the tech company I had cofounded (see the Preface for more detail). I joined the Reuters Digital Vision Program at Stanford for the 2004–2005 academic year, working with fifteen other fellows on projects combining technology and social benefit to the developing world. I joined forces with the Grameen Foundation on their open-source project for microfinance called Mifos (see Chapter 9, or www.mifos.org, for more detail). I was able to use my software project-management skills to make a tangible difference in a project used in microfinance institutions in Asia, Africa, and the Middle East, serving more than a quarter million borrowers. In addition to the sense of accomplishment from the Mifos project, I learned a lot during that year from the other fellows, and developed strong friendships with them.

I recently completed my second gap year, which started in April 2011. The idea for this book had been percolating, but I was making little progress on it when I tried to work on it in conjunction with my consulting practice. The space afforded by time away from regular employment has allowed me to devote myself to refining my thoughts, writing the text, and working with others to collect the stories you've read throughout this book.

Many high school students are considering taking a gap year as well, choosing to defer college admissions for a year after they graduate from high school. They may want a change of pace before launching into another four or more years of rigorous study, or perhaps they're not convinced college is the right next step in their life journey. Increasingly, colleges are supporting students' decisions to take some time before matriculating, especially if they do something meaningful in the interim, increasing their maturity and perspective. If a student is prepared to commit to a full year of volunteering with a single assignment, there are organizations offering placements overseas, teaching English, helping with community development, or interning in a nonprofit office. City Year (www.cityyear.org) offers ten-month service projects focused on keeping students in school in twenty-one U.S. cities with higher dropout rates. It's open to youth aged seventeen to twenty-four, with a high school degree or GED.

Each of the websites I listed in the Volunteering Vacations section also offers advice for those intending to spend a full year volunteering. In addition, there are books appealing specifically to this group of young adults:

* *The Complete Guide to the Gap Year: The Best Things to Do between High School and College* by Kristin M. White (2009).
* *Lonely Planet: The Gap Year Book* by Joe Bindloss, Charlotte Hindle, and Andrew Dean Nystrom (2005).
* *Gap Years for Grown Ups: The Most Comprehensive, Practical Guide from the Leading Gap Year Specialist* by Susan Griffith (2011, 4th edition).

The last book on this list points out that gap years aren't exclusively for young adults: people changing careers, starting retirement, or taking a sabbatical can also make an extended commitment to volunteer before starting the next phase of their life.

Recognition and Motivation

All of us like to know our work is valued. A word of appreciation goes a long way, especially if it's personal and specific, and shows how our contribution has made a real difference for others. Children are just like adults in this respect, and appreciate being recognized for their contributions too. Receiving acknowledgment from adults such as the project leaders or representatives of the organization can be a special thrill. (If your project leaders seem too busy

The Power of Music to Spread Environmental Concern

When Al Gore invited environmentalists from around the world to Nashville for an important update on the state of our environment, among the youngest was thirteen-year-old Aitan Grossman. How had Aitan earned such a coveted invitation?

After reading Mr. Gore's *An Inconvenient Truth* in third grade, Aitan hatched a plan to use the power of music and youth to spread Mr. Gore's urgent message. He composed the song "100 Generations," and through a nonprofit he created (www.kidEarth.us) coordinated kids performing it all around the world. By the time news of Aitan's project hit Mr. Gore's desk, Aitan's project had gone viral, reaching hundreds of thousands of people from more than one hundred countries.

Aitan's vision was simple: Engage the people who have most to lose—kids—in a medium that speaks to them the loudest—music. Aitan's unique and creative approach to this very serious problem sparked the media's interest and reached adults too, who couldn't help but take note of the kids' musical environmental pleas.

When not updating kidEarth's website with videos kids send of themselves singing "100 Generations," Aitan takes his song on the road to schools and conferences. There he combines his spirited message with Mr. Gore's somber one, just to make doubly sure the world knows what's in store if we don't act soon.

to notice, or aren't comfortable relating to children, a discreet prompt doesn't hurt.) Of course, children also appreciate praise from their parents, and it's appropriate to be lavish with it, whether the volunteer project was something your children initiated or something they joined reluctantly.

To encourage repeat volunteering, I encourage you to track the projects you and your children have worked on. Something as simple as the giving-back binder or notebook or a sticker chart is sufficient. If you'd like a more elaborate scrapbook devoted to volunteering, *The Giving Book* (Sabin, 2004) is a spiral-bound book with some questions to provoke children from seven to nine years old to reflect on service, with space to record pictures and notes about volunteering experiences. Be sure to take pictures of your involvement on volunteer projects you can save in your child's volunteering book. If you and your child feel comfortable, you can submit the pictures for publication, along with a brief article about what you did. The organization you helped might have a

newsletter that updates their supporters. If not, a church newsletter, neighborhood newsletter, or local newspaper might find the story newsworthy. Sharing
the photos and story online through a blog or social network can also keep
family and friends updated about your volunteering adventures (though keep
in mind privacy and safety considerations, especially when publishing your
child's name and photo).

CHAPTER 6

Donating with Children

How can we expect our children to know and experience the joy of giving unless we teach them that the greater pleasure in life lies in the art of giving rather than receiving?

—James Cash Penney, founder, J. C. Penney Company

Involving children in the financial side of giving helps in their growth and their understanding of money. The notion of sharing material wealth with those in need can be understood as soon as it becomes clear that money is a means to acquire things. Saving for future needs, giving to help others, and spending for current wants: This three-part understanding of money is within the reach of most five- or six-year-old children. A savings bank with three different slots—corresponding to saving, giving, and spending—makes this point directly.

In the same way adults have rules about enforced saving (whether self-imposed, such as a payroll deduction for retirement, or government-imposed, like the Social Security tax), it's appropriate for parents to set up rules for enforcing the allocation of money for their children. If you give your child an allowance, specifying the breakdown among the three categories of saving, giving, and spending is a way to help your child learn important budgeting skills. Extending that policy to money received as a gift from relatives or earned from chores or in other paid employment is a family choice, though having a consistent policy is a wise idea. As children get older, it's reasonable to offer more flexibility as they demonstrate greater understanding of the tradeoffs involved in their financial choices.

If giving money is too abstract, giving physical things is more immediate. Going through your family's closets and your kids' old games and giving the clothes and toys that you no longer use to an organization like Goodwill or the Salvation Army is a good idea. It helps reduce the clutter in your own home and lets other people make use of your family's outgrown clothes and toys. Involving your children in the decision about what to give away can serve as an early lesson in generosity. The idea that something that was "mine" is no longer can be a tough concept for some children to accept. You may find it frustrating that they're unwilling to part with their tricycles, even though they've been on two-wheelers for a year. As you explain to them the impracticality of hanging on to everything, remember to apply the same standard to your own things. How many small appliances are in the upper cupboard in the kitchen that you haven't used in the last three years? How many suits are in your closet that are still in good shape but you don't wear because they fit better when you were fifteen pounds lighter? Make a pact with your kids that each of you will reduce the stuff you have and, by giving it away, will help others who don't have as much as you do. It's also a good time to consider your purchasing habits: Do you buy things without considering how long they'll be useful or whether they're really needed at all? Disciplined spending, searching for bargains, and borrowing rather than buying are all habits you can teach your child and model in your own behavior to help them make the most of their financial resources.

Two aspects of involving children in financial giving stand out: One involves decisions concerning the family's giving; the second entails giving from their own resources.

If you're participating in family discussions around giving back, the Listening & Learning Conversation #2 (found in Chapter 7) will give everyone in your family an opportunity to voice thoughts about which groups to support. As your children consider their personal allocation, and describe their rationales, they're helping to influence the family decisions. Taking their input seriously means weighing their requests along with the causes and organizations you're predisposed to support as you make choices around the family's giving. It's also important that your children understand the way the final decision is going to be made, and respect the outcome, so you'll need to be prepared to make a compelling case describing your rationale.

Giving from your children's own resources is a different matter: Once they reach an age where they can make a reasonable evaluation, at nine or ten years old, they can be allowed to choose which groups will receive their support. You may want to encourage them to think seriously about their gifts by making their choices more significant. One way to increase the significance of their choices is by creating a matching gift: In the same way that some companies match the charitable contributions their employees make, you can offer to match the gifts your children choose to make. If they discover that the $20 they have saved will amount to a $60 or $100 gift with a two-to-one or a four-to-one match, they may be more excited about choosing which organization will receive their no-longer-so-modest gift. As their pattern of giving is established (and their earning power goes up), you can choose to ratchet back the ratio at which you match their gifts, or eliminate it entirely.

A second approach to giving children a taste of the excitement of helping others financially is to underwrite their gift entirely. You can give a gift certificate for a donation in their name to a charity of their choice, or use a website that allows them to give online. Although their gift will be restricted to a particular cause and organization, sites like Kiva (www.kiva.org) and DonorsChoose (www.donorschoose.org) allow children to choose a microentrepreneur or classroom project to fund. Global Giving (www.global-giving.org) uses a single gift card that can be redeemed for any of the hundreds projects on their site (cards expire in one year; the only cost above the donated

---

Teen Sponsors Dominican Child

Vicki was surprised when her thirteen-year-old daughter Alexa came home from school with a flyer for Children International and said she was going to sponsor a girl in the Dominican Republic. Although their family had been involved in volunteering and fundraising for activities ranging from school to church to sports, everything else had been local projects and concerns. Alexa's involvement was no short-lived teen fad. Over the years, she continued to support her Dominican *little sister* each month, sending money she earned from babysitting and other odd jobs for neighbors. She went beyond the minimum requirement, adding holiday gifts—carefully chosen clothing and things she knew her little sister would like, as well as extra money to help provide gifts for the children sponsored by people who hadn't been as thoughtful.

When Alexa heard that Children International was ceasing their support of all the children from her little sister's town, she was indignant. It was only after she had grilled the Children International officials and been convinced the transition was being handled well that she agreed to sponsor a different child in the newly opened areas. Alexa's relationship with her little siblings in the Dominican Republic has continued, with her parents Vicki and Mike agreeing to continue the sponsorship while Alexa is in college. The family has talked about making a postgraduation trip to the Dominican Republic to visit the "extended family," in what will surely be a memory-making experience to shape the reunion stories for years to come.

Eight-Year-Old Dedicates Birthday Gifts to Food Bank

Asked how a single mom with two active kids found time to volunteer on the weekends, Zeina replied that she kept weekends free for family time—no sports, music, or anything with weekly practices or games on the weekends. Volunteering was possible on the weekend because it *was* family time. She was actively looking for (and encouraging her employer to provide) more opportunities where she and her children could volunteer together. "We feel closer when we do things together," she said. In her search for opportunities, she found Project Linus, where her children made no-sew fleece blankets, and Collective Roots, a public gardening project.

For one of the volunteer projects, the family worked with Second Harvest Food Bank, helping to pack food boxes for delivery to different aid organizations in the area. It had such an impact on seven-year-old Maya that when her next birthday arrived, she decided to ask her birthday guests to give money to Second Harvest Food Bank rather than bring gifts. Impressed by the generosity of such a young donor, Second Harvest responded by recognizing Maya with a certificate and an apron with the Second Harvest logo.

amount is for expedited shipping of physical cards). Network for Good (www.networkforgood.org) also has a gift card for making donations to the 1.2 million charities on the site (there's a $5 processing fee above the amount of the card, which expires in six months). Some donor-advised funds (see Chapter 11) also offer gift certificates allowing the recipient to choose which organization receives the money.

Children can have their very own donor-advised fund through the website YouthGive (www.youthgive.org). Parents sign up for the account, and fund it with an initial donation, which is tax-deductible. Other friends and relatives can be authorized to add to it as well. The child then makes disbursements from the account to his or her selection from the Giving Menu, a growing list of more than one hundred nonprofit organizations (predominantly California-based, though some with a global focus). The organizations are proposed and profiled by the youth themselves. There are no fees associated with the accounts, and 100 percent of the donations are passed along to the chosen grantee.

Grandparents and other relatives can spur giving by including such a gift card as part of a birthday or other holiday gift. (It's a good idea to check in with the parents first, to see how it fits in with the family's charitable plans.)

If a child gets really excited about raising money for a chosen cause, you could suggest throwing their birthday party in honor of the organization, so guests make donations to the charity rather than bringing gifts.* Such generosity is rare among children (and adults), and the local press may deem it newsworthy. If your child has made this decision, ask if he or she would like to tell the story to the newspaper to help other readers learn about and support the cause as well. You can help a child recognize the power of his or her voice at an early age, and show the persuasive force such an example provides. That type of empowerment may set children on an early path to leadership in activism.

---

* The website www.cloverbyclover.com provides the structure for a child to set up a party/cause page, designate an organization to receive a percentage of the gifts, and potentially retain a percentage for him or herself to purchase a "single special gift." The administrative fee of 10 percent does cut into the gift amount, however. Although Jolkona Foundation (www.jolkona. org) isn't quite as kid-friendly, it does send 100 percent of gifts received to the designated cause.

CHAPTER 7

Volunteering Strategically

Our problem is not to find better values but to be faithful to those we profess.

—John W. Gardner, Secretary of Health, Education, and Welfare under President Lyndon Johnson

After an initial exposure to volunteering, by working with one organization or several, you may be ready to take the next step and engage more strategically in your volunteering with nonprofits. Doing so will enable:

❖ Sustained help to a single organization, with a better understanding of their mission, methods, and beneficiaries.

❖ The opportunity to take a leadership role as a project leader, staff member, or director.

❖ The potential to launch your own project or organization implementing your ideas for making the world a better place.

❖ Deeper familiarity with the financial aspects of the organization, with the opportunity to see how a more significant donation would have a strategic impact.

Narrowing Your Focus and Going Deeper

If your earlier volunteering experiences have been about getting a broad overview of different causes and approaches, strategic volunteering is about narrowing your focus to the topics that are most meaningful to you and going deep.

Exercise: Snapshot of Your Current Giving Back

1. Take a minute to review the causes and organizations you currently support with your giving. The following table with sample answers will show

GIVING-BACK SNAPSHOT

Organization	Cause	Avg. $/year	Avg. hours/ year	Specific Talents Used	Assessment
Big Brothers	Youth Development	60	100	Mentoring	Very good. Like direct impact.
Town soccer league	Youth Development	150	80	Soccer	Starting to lose interest.
Sierra Club	Environment	500	0	n/a	Like their conservation programs.
College	Education	250	0	n/a	Obligation gift.
Church	Religion	700	120	Singing	Excellent sense of community.
Totals		1,660	300		

you how to collect the information in one place. (You can download a blank grid for the exercise at www.giving-back.info.)

2. Once you've filled out a similar table of your own, review the results, looking for trends.

❖ Are you concentrating all your efforts in one organization? Multiple organizations working on the same cause? One geographic area?

❖ Have you chosen to take on greater responsibility over time? Are you using your talents in some of your giving-back projects?

❖ Do you support organizations with gifts across multiple categories (monetary, time, skill, and connections)?

❖ How do you feel about the gifts you're making? Are they appreciated by the organization? Do you think they make a difference for the organization? Are you benefiting from them by learning new skills, meeting new people, or seeing how your gifts affect the beneficiaries? Are you proud to be associated with the organization?

3. Finally, think about how you selected these organizations for your giving back.

   ❖ Do you think you knew enough about the organizations before you committed to working with them?

   ❖ Did you consider how each gift relates to the other gifts to complete a whole picture?

   ❖ Are you happy with the degree of concentration by cause, organization type, and gift type?

   ❖ Are the organizations best able to use your unique skills getting access to them?

   ❖ Overall, are you satisfied with the portfolio of giving you've assembled, or are there areas where you'd like to make changes?

Continuing the Review Process

If you're like most of us, this review process will uncover a hodgepodge of different commitments with several organizations you've supported in various ways over the years. Most likely, your volunteer activities have sprung up as people have asked you to help out, perhaps with an activity in your child's school or sports team or your church. What started out as a one-time commitment may have become an annual one when you were labeled "the person who was so good at running the cashier's table at the bake sale." Your financial giving probably reflects a bit of a patchwork as well, perhaps support for a friend who was raising money for Team in Training, a gift to the American Cancer Society in memory of a relative who passed away, and your response to a Red Cross appeal for the latest natural disaster.

This chapter is meant to jumpstart the exploration process to help you find the causes most important to you. You'll have a chance to think about the forces that helped you grow, the things that occupy your attention today, and your hopes for the future. As you delve deeper into these topics, you'll likely discover the values that are central to who you are and what you'd like to become. Spending time with people who share those values and want to spread them will generate energy and passion, and can lead to a sense of fulfillment as your own efforts spread those values.

If you're making a family project of developing a giving-back strategy, the values-discovery section in this chapter will serve as the basis for the first of the Listening & Learning Conversations, found later in the chapter.

Values Discovery: The Past

For most of us, our parents had the greatest influence in shaping our lives during the formative childhood years. They created our home environment. They exposed us to different learning opportunities through books, television, school, playdates, trips, and family outings. They helped us make sense of the world and disciplined us when we crossed certain lines. They answered us each time we asked why, and by their example we made our judgments about what was good and normal in the world. Of course, it wasn't always our biological mother and father exclusively who raised us. Other caregivers, relatives, and teachers exerted their influence as well. As we grew up, we turned to friends and public or historical figures as role models whose opinions we valued and tended to make our own.

Take some time to think about the following questions, even writing out your answers to them. If you're doing this exercise as a family, I suggest saving the more detailed stories for another time, and keeping the Listening & Learning Conversation answers more concise. With several people all sharing their answers to these questions, many of the interesting anecdotes will have to come later.

Considering the Past

Answer each of these questions with a few sentences. Where the question brings to mind longer stories, jot down some key phrases that tell the highlights of those stories. Use your giving-back notebook to record your answers for these questions and the subsequent discussions and exercises. As you pursue your practice of strategic volunteering, you'll enjoy looking back to see how you got started and how your views have changed along the way. A sample answer set appears later in the chapter, along with the extraction of key values from it.

❖ Where did you grow up? Feel free to interpret this question however you like: Your answer might be a geographical location (New York City) or a setting (around my grandmother's kitchen table) or something more abstract (in the world of books). The key point is to think about the important circumstances during your childhood.

❖ What groups or organizations (aside from your family) were most influential in your upbringing?

❖ When did you feel like you were first taken seriously? What was the organization or cause where you felt your opinions were listened to, and you could influence the outcome through your efforts or leadership?

❖ What activities did you do with your parents that you remember most fondly?

A Poster Comes to Life

"My son Will and I and some of his high school friends were interested in serving by exploring the connections between popular clothing stores and the conditions where the clothes were made. We had learned from national campaign material that our local stores were selling fashionable clothes manufactured by young people in factories in Central America and Southeast Asia that were considered sweatshops.

"So my son and his friends and I volunteered to leaflet with signs in front of one local clothing retailer to raise questions about young people working in sweatshop conditions overseas. One poster we carried showed a particularly courageous-looking young woman who worked in a clothing factor in El Salvador. Our leafleting was successful in informing shoppers, and some decided not to shop in the store.

"Later that year, my son and I joined an international service trip to El Salvador to learn firsthand from the experience of bringing donations and visiting community organizations we had supported. One of the organizations we visited was involved in the sweatshop campaign. We entered the meeting room for a conversation about the campaign, and who should walk in but the young woman whose picture we had featured in our posters! When we described how we knew her face and the small way we had shown our support, she burst into tears and embraced the young people in our group. Suddenly the assertions behind the sweatshop campaign became very real as our poster came to life. We even visited the poor community where she and her family lived.

"Several years later, Gap, in response to persistent consumer questions, changed their policies and began to require compliance with a code of conduct by their third-party suppliers. The memory of that face-to-face meeting with the young woman in El Salvador has stayed with us ever since."

—Leif Erickson, Executive Director,
Youth Community Service (www.youthcommunityservice.org),
a Palo Alto, California, service organization

Values Discovery: The Present

The way you live today is also a statement of your values. You may be conscious of compromises preventing you from living out your values fully, but hopefully the choices you make are consistent with your most important values. The work you do, the people you associate with, and the activities you engage in outside of work are all choices representing your values.

Considering the Present

Answer each of these questions with a few sentences. Where the question brings to mind longer stories, jot down some key phrases that tell the highlights of those stories.

* What groups are you proud of belonging to?
* What do you do that brings you joy or expresses your creativity?
* What family activities bring you closer together?
* When you travel, whether in your own neighborhood or around the world, what groups do you see that are treated unfairly or need extra help?

Values Discovery: The Future

Much of our giving back is focused on making the world a better place for future generations. Visualize the conditions you'd like to pass on to your children and their descendants. Consider what problems humanity could eliminate today, and which ones future generations will still need to contend with. Which values could be instilled that will lead to flourishing in the future? What good aspects of the world today are in danger of being lost or forgotten?

Considering the Future

Answer each of these questions with a few sentences. Where the question brings to mind longer stories, jot down some key phrases that tell the highlights of those stories.

* What problems facing the world today would you most like to see solved?
* What aspect of your heritage is most important to conserve for the future?
* Are there any local groups doing a good job of preparing your neighborhood or town for the future? What problems are they addressing?
* What one invention or discovery would improve your quality of life the most?

Exercise: Extracting the Important Values

Look through your answers to all three sections on values discovery—past, present, and future—for common themes. Are there organizations or activities that show up repeatedly? What about higher-level values like an appreciation for nature, education, or religion? Take the one value or theme that seems the most prevalent, circle the words or concepts related to it, and count how many times that value or topic occurs. Repeat that process for the second- and third-most-common topics. Does that list seem to be a good summary of

VALUES-DISCOVERY WORKSHEET

The Past

Where did you grow up? *As a math teaching assistant in college*

What groups or organizations (aside from your family) were most influential in your upbringing? *Boy Scouts, Youth Soccer Team*

When did you feel like you were first taken seriously? What was the organization or cause where you felt that your opinions were listened to, and you could influence the outcome through your efforts or leadership?
As Editor of the HS Yearbook

What activities did you do with your parents that you remember most fondly?
Lake Summer vacation; Baking Christmas cookies

The Present

What groups are you proud of belonging to? *Big Brothers*

What do you do that brings you joy or expresses your creativity?
Hiking; Playing jazz piano

What family activities bring you closer together? *DisneyLand Trips*

When you travel, whether in your own neighborhood or around the world, what groups do you see that are treated unfairly or need extra help?
Autistic children; disabled veterans

The Future

What problems facing the world today would you most like to see solved?
Global warming, Hunger/Famine in Africa

What aspect of your heritage is most important to conserve for the future?
Civil War memorials

Are there any local groups doing a good job of preparing your neighborhood or town for the future? What problems are they addressing?
PTA: Funding for sports and arts in schools

What one invention or discovery would improve your quality of life the most?
A cure for cancer

Top 3 Common themes:

Education/Mentoring:	Environment/Nature:	Medical Research:
THI I	III	II

your most important values? (You can download a blank grid for the exercise at www.giving-back.info.)

Family Discussion

Now we'll move to the first of the family discussions, focused on the values-discovery explorations you've just done. (If you're reading the book as an individual, feel free to skip ahead to p. 73.) Through this conversation, you'll learn more about what your family members view as most important. Explicitly naming those values, and thinking about ways you can directly put them into practice, can be a powerful exercise spurring you to action. Along the way, you'll likely share some fond memories about important events, people, and places in your life, and build family memories of your own as you hold your first Listening & Learning Conversation.

Listening & Learning Conversation #1
Shared-Values Discovery

If you're working together with other family members to create a giving plan, Listening & Learning Conversation #1 will give you a chance to share your answers to values-discovery questions and listen to the responses of the rest of your family. Refer back to p. 19 in Chapter 2 for the guidelines of a Listening & Learning conversation if you need to.

Each of you has reflected about your values on your own, doing your best to identify them and see where they came from, how they're reflected in your life today, and how you hope to see them play out in the world of the future. Now it's time to hear what others in your family said.

Conversation Goals

1. *Establish shared commitment:* Establish a shared commitment for treating one another respectfully and working together. Your overall goal is to understand your family's practice of giving back and evaluate whether and how to change it.

2. *Share:* Share the answers to the questions that you worked on independently.

3. *Notice commonalities and differences:* Look to see where there are commonalities and differences.

General Flow of Conversation

1. *Kicking off:* As the person who suggested reading this book and doing the exercises as a family, share why you wanted to do it. Express appreciation for others' willingness to join in, explicitly acknowledging that you're giving everyone a voice in the process, and that there isn't a predetermined "right answer." While it would be great if there's something the whole family is fired up about, it's fine if not everyone wants to be involved in the final plan, or if the final plan has different parts people work on separately.

2. *Sharing answers for questions about past and present:* Since the content is related, it's easier for each person to cover both sections during the first turn. It's fine to read the answers to the questions as you've written them, or you can start with the list of the top values so it's easier for the listeners to identify them. When the first person has finished, let the next person share his or her responses, until you've all spoken.

3. *Sharing answers for questions about future:* Make a second pass around the circle, giving each person a chance to talk about hopes for the future, as described in the responses to the third set of questions.

4. *Commenting on each person's responses:* Make a third pass around the circle where each person is invited to make a short comment on what he or she found most interesting about the responses to the questions from each of the family members. These comments are intended to be encouraging and positive, highlighting something the speaker learned about each person from his or her answers.

5. *Summarizing commonalities:* Open the conversation up for anyone to show where the different family members came up with similar responses. Look especially for overlap among the top three values each of you mentioned. The values common to several or all of the family members are likely to be the starting points for selecting causes and organizations you can all support enthusiastically.

6. *Concluding the conversation:* Make one final pass around the circle where each member says what he or she liked most or found most memorable about the conversation. Thank one another for their attention, and plan when to hold the next Listening & Learning Conversation.

Special Notes for Parents

Since your children have had less life experience, they may have less to say, and the prospect of participating in a "serious conversation" with parents may cause them to hold back or be shy. Do your best to draw them out if necessary, and ask followup questions showing you're interested in what they have to say and value their input into this family discussion. By the same token, you and your spouse have had more time and might be more comfortable answering these questions. Remember to avoid monopolizing the conversation, and be careful not to repeat stories that might generate a there-they-go-again reaction from your children.

Special Notes for Children

This conversation is about the things that are important to you. When you give your answers, try to explain why you selected each. It may be easier to remember things that happened recently, but try to remember things that were longer ago too. Remember to use the yellow card if you think someone is talking too long, or the red one if you hear an argument starting.

Reflecting on the Conversation

After the first Listening & Learning Conversation has ended, take some time to reflect on the conversation and the process so far. As you evaluate your thoughts about it, you'll also come up with some ideas on how future conversations can be more productive.

Review the following questions, and summarize your answers briefly.

Overall Conversation

❖ Did you meet the goal of everyone listening to and understanding one another's answers to the questions?

❖ Did you finish in a reasonable amount of time?

❖ Were you able to work together to identify common family values?

❖ Did each person get a fair share of the overall time?

❖ Was everyone treated with respect?

❖ Did you follow the guidelines for Listening & Learning Conversations?

❖ When people were carded, were the objections appropriate? Did they modify their behavior as requested?

❖ Was the room and setting comfortable for the discussion?

Family Values
- ❖ What were the most consistent themes judging by what family members shared?
- ❖ Were there any values that showed up on everyone's list?
- ❖ What did you hear that surprised you?
- ❖ Which of your important values require more work to ensure they're passed on to others?
- ❖ What values do you admire in other family members and want to try to adopt?
- ❖ Were there any values or topics other people felt so passionately about that you'd like to support them, even if it's not a core value you hold yourself?
- ❖ How are you changed as a result of having this conversation?
- ❖ What would you like your family to do differently for future Listening & Learning Conversations?
- ❖ What topics or points would you like to hear more about?

Setting Priorities

Now that you've had a chance to explore your values more deeply, whether as an individual or as a family, it's time to look at how to translate your values into actions in ways that fit in with the rest of your life.

Exercise: Prioritizing Your Activities

Odds are that you have more things you'd like to do than you have time to do. This exercise will help you prioritize to make sure you're devoting your scarce time to the activities that yield the best payoff for advancing your chosen causes.

Needed for This Exercise

- ❖ Twenty nickels (or twenty $5 Monopoly bills)
- ❖ Three slips of paper, labeled with the top three causes from your values-discovery exercise

Setup

1. Place the three slips of paper on the table, each separated by several inches. Below each heading, place nickels according to this provisional allocation:
   * Cause number one, ten nickels (50¢)
   * Cause number two, six nickels (30¢)
   * Cause number three, four nickels (20¢)

Process

2. Imagine that the coins represent the time you have to allocate to these different causes. In the initial setup, your time is divided among the three different causes with more weight given to the ones you'd identified as more important. Does that represent your interests? If not, move the coins around, giving those you feel deserve more of your time additional coins and taking coins away from the less compelling causes. It's fine if you decide some of the topics don't get any coins at all. If the other causes are more important to you, it's better to focus on them than to spread yourself too thin.

3. Continue moving the coins around until the money assigned to each cause represents the importance of spending your time working on that cause.

Reality Check

4. While it's tempting to support all the causes you care about, it may not be realistic given the amount of time you have available. Think about the number of hours you have available to give back by volunteering during the week. Multiply that number of hours by the percentage allocation (the number of cents you gave to each cause) to see how many hours each would get on a weekly basis. For example, if you had assigned "Treatment of Animals" a 10 percent allocation, and you have four hours to give each week, that would only amount to about twenty-five minutes per week. Driving to the local animal shelter may well take more than twenty-five minutes just to get there and back, leaving you no time at all to help with the volunteering.

   If you don't have enough time to contribute meaningfully on a weekly basis, consider devoting larger blocks of time less frequently (10 percent of your four hours a week adds up to about one and a half hours a month or twenty hours a year), which could be a great way to stay involved with a group and cause you care about. On the other hand, you may decide it just isn't feasible to make the numbers work: The time slice is too small, and the frequency isn't enough for you to feel engaged with the organization (or the organization may require that you commit more hours). In that case, it's better to acknowledge the reality of how much time you have to give, cross that organization off your list, and reallocate its time funds to another organization that ranked more highly in your allocation. Repeat this exercise with each of the causes in your top three. You could, of course, spend all your available time on the one project that is most important to you, but the variety of working with multiple organizations and the ability to share ideas across organizations or causes can also be fun and helpful.

Finding Your Niche

You can use your skills in many different ways to help the causes you care about. When we looked at possible roles for your initial volunteer experience in Chapter 3, the focus was on jobs that didn't require much training or integration with the organization, because you only had a few hours to commit. When you're willing to make a longer-term agreement to volunteer, more options open up. The organization will get a chance to know you and your work, and feel comfortable that you can be a reliable part of their team. Your interactions with them will demonstrate your capabilities, and they will consider whether a role with greater responsibility is appropriate. You may also be able to find an opportunity to try a new skill you'd like to develop. Bringing your passion, commitment, good intentions, and willingness to learn are the hallmarks of a good volunteer—one that any organization would be delighted to involve in their mission.

The following list summarizes the different types of positions or tasks you could do, along with some typical responsibilities for each.

- ❖ *Front lines:* Working directly with beneficiaries of an organization: serving in a soup kitchen, caring for animals in a shelter, removing invasive plants or tutoring students.
- ❖ *Back office:* Using administrative or creative skills to ensure the people on the front lines can work effectively: scheduling workdays, producing newsletters, designing a website or poster, or creating a budget and balancing the books.
- ❖ *Advocacy:* Changing the public opinion or the beliefs of key individuals to influence policy decisions: writing a letter to the editor or contacting a

reporter about a newsworthy story, visiting a senator or a senator's staffers, or writing a position paper to explain the organization's research and recommendations.

❖ **Fundraising:** Ensuring the organization has the financial resources to achieve its mission: writing grant applications to foundations, calling or meeting individuals to solicit gifts, asking local merchants for in-kind donations, organizing a dinner for donor prospects or a silent auction, or sending out a direct-mail campaign.

❖ **Research:** Developing new techniques for addressing the problem; creating scientific or organizational innovations to be shared by different organizations working on this problem.

❖ **Board of directors:** Creating the mission for the organization, evaluating the performance of the executive director and other paid staff, participating in fundraising, and recruiting other directors.[*]

Take a look and consider which roles are most interesting to you. It doesn't need to be the same for each organization or cause you work with. You might want to serve on the front lines with one organization, for example, working directly with teens on their job-interview skills; but with another, you'd prefer to create flyers and brush up on your desktop-publishing skills.

You'll need to be realistic about the types of roles you can perform given your time available. While most organizations can carve out smaller tasks for people who are able to volunteer only occasionally, those tasks are often limited in responsibility and typically fall into the front-lines and back-office categories. Advocacy and fundraising can be flexible: The more time you have, the more important a role you can play in sharing the message. These roles, however, require you to have a very high level of understanding about the organization and the cause, so typically they are limited to people who have gained quite a bit of experience volunteering with the organization. Working in a research capacity requires a substantial commitment. You're unlikely to be able to contribute to the research or even stay abreast of what others are doing if you aren't prepared to spend at least ten hours a week.

---

[*] BoardSource has a lot of information about the responsibilities of board members. See http://www.boardsource.org/Knowledge.asp?ID=3.368 for a list of ten responsibilities of the board of directors of a nonprofit.

Assuming a Leadership Role in an Organization

Given the huge challenges nonprofits are trying to tackle, often with limited financial resources and a mostly volunteer staff, talented leadership can make a huge difference. If you have the commitment and time to devote to giving back, think seriously about working your way up to a leadership role.

If you can answer yes to most of these questions, you're a good candidate for a leadership role:

* Is it important to know the leaders of the organization personally?
* Do you have time to make a significant commitment over several years?
* Are you comfortable talking to others about the cause and asking for help?
* Do you want to have say in key decisions?
* Are you willing to take responsibility if things aren't going well?
* Is it important to you to get credit if things do go well?
* Have you held leadership positions in the past?
* Are you comfortable working with budgets and raising money?

Given the many needs of nonprofits, they're often willing to give you significant responsibility if you demonstrate passion, commitment, and competence. If you have innate leadership talent, consider applying it in service of your chosen cause. You may even consider becoming a part of the paid staff, making it a career focus as well as a cause dear to your heart.

Parents Supporting Students' Service Ideas

Palo Alto's Gunn High School boasts what may be the only program of its kind in the United States: Gunn @ Your Service, a parent-sponsored, tax-exempt school boosters club that supports students' community service. Its mission is broad and innovative, featuring programs like Gunn Grants, a microgrant program encouraging student social entrepreneurs with money and mentors who support projects of the students' own design. One such grant provided seed funding for music books so Gunn students who give lessons in a low-income community could loan books to their students.

"Gunn @ Your Service is about making service easy for busy students and their families as well as creating positive associations with service our teens can carry with them for the rest of their lives. Our hope is that when Gunn students move to new communities they will continue volunteering or—better yet—start their own nonprofits and inspire other kids to serve too," according to Lauren Janov, Gunn @ Your Service's president.

In addition to the day-to-day leadership roles within the organization, the board of directors plays a key oversight role. Serving as a director on the board is typically a multiyear commitment, where you take on a fiduciary and legal responsibility. Talk with other directors from the board, and know what you're getting into before you agree to stand for election. Many boards require directors to help with fundraising. Some even have a "give or get" dollar expectation that directors will either donate themselves or find others to make contributions of thousands of dollars. On the other hand, serving as a director can be very fulfilling as you work with other smart, caring people on questions of strategic importance. Many organizations are in need of good board members, so once you have determined it's a position you're prepared to do and do well, consider meeting with a current director or other leader to express your interest in serving.

Giving Back with Your Network

In addition to your time, skills, and money, there's a valuable fourth way you can give back: with your network. Nearly every organization desires to spread its message to a broader audience. Having that message come from a friend is a very effective way to rise above the noise. Therefore, when you've reached a level of comfort with an organization—that is, you know that it's pursuing a good mission, using effective means, and operating in an efficient manner—think about which of your friends would be receptive to learning more about it. Sharing the word is a valuable service you can offer to the organization. A tech-savvy organization might have tools you can use to promote it on social-networking sites, coverage that can be re-tweeted and shared, potentially reaching thousands of people. Old-fashioned networking, by phone or in person, can be even more effective at enlisting new supporters. People respond well to a personal contact, especially when you describe why the opportunity is relevant to you, and to them. A personal appeal to a handful of truly interested people will generate more enthusiasm than a mass email to dozens.

Of course, it's important to be judicious with your messages so you don't overwhelm your friends and acquaintances with messages they weren't expecting. If you plan to broadcast often on behalf of an organization (or several), it's best to set up a separate account for those messages and ensure that the people on the list have opted in to receiving those communications, and that they have an easy way to opt out if they change their mind.

Exercise: Cause Inventory

This is a good point to stop and take stock of how far you've come. By reflecting on your values, the more practical matters of how and where you'd like to give back, and the causes and approaches you're drawn to, you've created a picture of the elements in your ideal giving-back scenario. Now you're ready for the future-looking version of the snapshot of your giving you composed at the start of this chapter.

By combining your current commitments with this ideal mix, you can identify the areas that don't match up: either an existing commitment that's no longer compelling, or a gap where you'd like to do more. Use a grid similar to the following sample chart to capture the areas where you'd like to increase your volunteer efforts. (You can download a blank grid for the exercise at www.giving-back.info.) Remember, here your focus is on your future intentions.

CAUSE-INVENTORY WORKSHEET				
Cause	Your Role	Specific Talents Used	Target Time Allocation	Current Time Allocation
Mentoring	Front Lines (Big Brother)	Leadership, Teaching	2 hours/wk	2 hours/wk
Medical Research	Fundraising (American Cancer Society)	Network, Social Media	4 hours/mo	0
Environment	Back Office (Acterra)	Graphic Design (Annual report)	8 hours/yr	0

If other members of the family are participating in the discussions of your giving-back plan, the cause-inventory checkpoint is a good time to have Listening & Learning Conversation #2, where each member of the family discusses the causes that he or she feels strongly about, and the ideal ways for giving back. Later, Chapter 8 will give you a framework for thinking more deeply about how the organizations you work with (or you start) can have a larger impact, and Chapter 9 (extending the work you did in Chapter 3) helps you structure the research to find the best partner organizations for you. (Feel free to skip ahead to p. 86 if you're using the book as an individual.)

Listening & Learning Conversation #2 Looking for Common Ground

By now each of you has done a lot of thinking about which causes are most important to you and how you might support them since you shared the thoughts about your values in Listening & Learning Conversation #1. As you come back together as a family, your goal is to both share the thinking you've done and listen to the ideas from your other family members. It's unlikely you'll all have reached the same level of detail in your thinking or that there's enough agreement to immediately start working together on the ultimate family project. Looking for the areas of common ground is the theme of this conversation. What areas present enough overlap to explore further for that ideal family project? Does it seem there's not much commonality, and maybe the best plan is to provide encouragement, supporting one another in the different projects you're each doing independently? Or are there ways to come together?

Conversation Goals

1. *Share:* Share your personal passion for the causes, level, and type of giving back you feel most called to do.

2. *Listen:* Hear the same from each family member.

3. *Evaluate:* Evaluate the potential for collaborative projects.

4. *Set a plan:* Set a plan for researching and contacting organizations.

General Flow of Conversation

1. *Sharing:* Starting with the youngest, have each person spend a few minutes talking about their top two interests:
   - Cause
   - Geography
   - What role you'd like to play in helping, including specific skills, if applicable
   - Tentative ideas about organizations you think may be interesting
   - The percentage of available time you allocated to this cause

❖ For example: "I'm concerned about the environment, and the effects of global warming. While it's a global problem, I'm interested in things we can do locally, in our own town. I think if more people understood the impact their driving had on the environment, they would cut down on the number of miles they drove. It would be neat to use my artistic skills to make a difference. I'm also disappointed that some of the poorer kids in nearby schools don't have any books at home. I love to read, and I'd like to make sure every child has the chance to read with their parents. The reading project seems more important to me, but I'm not sure how I could help."

2. *Offering encouragement:* Let each person take a minute to respond to the presentation, mentioning overlap between his or her own list and what was just presented. This is the time for each person to offer some form of encouragement to the presenter. For example, can you think of other examples of how the person has already been involved in helping that cause, or is already using the skills that he or she mentioned (or, even better, skills he or she might not have noticed that could help the cause)?

3. *Finding common ground:* After all family members have covered their own views, it's time to look for common ground. The parents can take the lead here, unless they feel the children are ready to assume the responsibility for this challenging task. Taking into account everything you've heard, what do you think is the relative level of common ground within the family?

Very High: The same causes were mentioned by everyone, along with agreement on the geography for helping. There was enthusiasm about working together, and you were finishing one another's sentences. Great! This case is most likely to lead to a successful, fulfilling collaboration with your family. Your shared enthusiasm can help keep everyone going when one of you gets discouraged or is having a harder time keeping up. With agreement on the cause and geography, it's likely you'll be able to agree on a research plan and choose the final action plan in the next conversation.

High: A single cause appeared in the top two for all the children, and was either highly ranked by the adults or they are willing to compromise and adopt the younger generation's interest for the sake of working together. As with the prior category, it looks like there's a viable plan for collaborating on a single family project. Take time to further develop the compromise plan, and, with luck, as you dig deeper into it, excitement will build and everyone will be eager to work together.

Moderate: Although there wasn't a single cause you were all willing to come together on, each child had at least one of his or her causes that was an interest (or an acceptable compromise) for a parent too. In this case, it's less likely that the family will all end up working on a single project. During the next research phase, spend the time developing the different options. It may turn out that a more avid researcher can bring one of the ideas to life, convincing the rest of you to join as well. On the other hand, it's fine to have multiple projects underway. To prepare for the action plan, have a sponsor for each cause take charge of leading the research and proposal.

Low: There was a difference in opinions among the family members, and not everyone's desires could be accommodated. In particular, some child doesn't have an adult willing to work together on his or her project. As in the previous case, there will be multiple research efforts going on. The child who had the singular interest could either pursue it independently (especially if he or she is a mature tween or teen), but, realistically, without the help of an adult for transportation and mentoring, the chances of a successful experience are limited. Either at this stage or during the next Listening & Learning Conversation, it's better to try to recruit that child for one of the other projects.

4. *Planning for the next stage:* Depending on the level of overlap among the family members as measured earlier, you'll be developing an action plan to get involved in one or more projects to give back. Pick a date for the next Listening & Learning Conversation, and select a sponsor for each project, who will lead the effort (with others' help) to prepare the research described in the next two chapters.

5. *Celebrating:* Take a few minutes to appreciate how much you've learned about yourselves and your family during this process. This self-discovery and sharing will go a long way toward helping you understand and appreciate one another more.

Special Notes for Parents

Here again, your role is a balancing act. In general, the more you can let your children lead this conversation, the more invested they'll be in the outcome, and the more likely you'll all be able to follow through with the momentum needed to make the plans happen. However, if your children are younger or less comfortable taking an assertive role, you'll need to lead the way, engaging your children to the greatest extent possible. Make sure everyone's ideas are discussed, everyone's opinions are heard, decisions are made, and clear expectations are set for the next meeting, including what each person will do to prepare for it.

On the flip side, if your child gets excited about the topic and starts making unrealistic plans, it's your job to bring the voice of reason and experience to the situation. Doing so may be viewed as being uncooperative or uncommitted, so you need to raise your concerns in a diplomatic way to have the desired effect of reining in the scope to something achievable. It's better to moderate the initial enthusiasm rather than set up a future failure by choosing an unattainable goal. If possible, provide coaching that expresses support for the child's openhearted desire to help, while still leading to a more reasonable level of commitment. For example, "It's great you'd like to give back five hours a week, but that's a lot to add to our schedule. Maybe we can start slower, with, say, two hours per week, and build up as we see how it's working out, and whether it fits in with homework." Ask if there's another activity that the child would consider giving up if the volunteering turns out to be a fulfilling direction.

After spending time evaluating your own interests, you may be disappointed if your children are moved by entirely different causes. Hold your ideas lightly, so that if your children's ideas are something that they feel strongly about, you can choose to support them and their ideas first. After all, helping your children to develop these areas of leadership and self-identity is a key part of this process, and the opportunity to bond over a cause your son or daughter is passionate about is a great gift. You'll still be able to pursue your own interests, and you can follow up even more deeply on your own passions when you enter the empty-nester phase.

Special Notes for Children

This conversation is an opportunity for you to demonstrate your maturity. In it, you'll show you can help create a plan for working together with your parents. Hopefully, you've gotten excited thinking about ways you can give back. That excitement will be needed to carry out your plans. As your family makes plans, realize the ideas you're proposing will have a big impact on your parents too. They will need to be involved: volunteering alongside you, changing mealtimes to accommodate a volunteering schedule, maybe providing rides for you. Listen carefully if they raise concerns about how it can all work out. Express appreciation for the things they already do to make your life easier. Work together to think through how you can all make the everyday things function more smoothly so there's more time to give back. Recognize that the causes that are most important to you might not be the same as theirs, and they may be sacrificing their own interests to support yours.

Reflecting on the Conversation

Take some time to think about your answers to the following questions and summarize them by writing a few sentences. Review your thoughts before the next Listening & Learning Conversation to help use the time as effectively as possible.

Overall Conversation
* Did you meet the goal of everyone listening to and understanding one another's answers to the questions?
* Did you finish in a reasonable amount of time?
* Were you able to work together to identify common family causes?
* Did each person get a fair share of the overall time?
* Was everyone treated with respect?
* Did you follow the guidelines for a Listening & Learning Conversation?
* When people were carded, were the objections appropriate? Did they modify their behavior as requested?
* Was the room and setting comfortable for the discussion?

Family Causes

- What were the most consistent themes judging by what family members shared?
- Were there any causes that showed up on everyone's list?
- What did you hear that surprised you?
- What causes and ideas did other members of my family bring up that you want to learn more about?
- Were there any causes or ideas other people felt so passionately about that you'd like to support them?
- How are you changed as a result of this conversation?
- What would you like your family to do differently for future Listening & Learning Conversations?
- What topics or points would you like to hear more about?

Stanford Grads Lead Building of Hospital in India

Five twenty-something Stanford alumni, united by their student volunteering experience in India over the course of a decade, hatched a plan to help meet one of the key needs for the Indian state of Jharkhand: local medical care. Nearly one hundred thousand villagers have to travel three hours or more to get to the hospital at the state capital. Building a local health center would provide timely care that could save lives and double as a community center for health-education programs. Despite their busy professional lives and living spread out across the United States, the cofounders of Hospital for Hope (www.hospitalforhope.org) kept at their dream. They started off by raising more than $100,000 for the construction costs through their online efforts, happy hours, and gala events, learning to partner with other nonprofits to pull together the large events. They worked with One World Children's Fund (their fiscal agent), Construction for Change (to do the building), and Jagriti Vihara (JV), the local non-governmental organization that will work with other community partners to run the hospital.

With the initial money raised and construction underway, the Hospital for Hope team has entered a new phase, planning for the staffing, operations, and ensuring the sustainability of the hospital. Now taking the role of consultants to JV, they've researched the best models for hospitals in developing areas, along with pitfalls to avoid. The project has provided valuable real-world experience in all the skills required to carry out a complex project: visioning and planning, implementation, partnering, and management. These skills have transferred to their day jobs, but the most valuable part of their volunteer experience was the inspiration of working with people so committed to helping others. As cofounder Golda Philip says, "We were searching for what we wanted to do, a sense of purpose and vocation. JV gave us a model. . . . It provided inspiration for all of us at an early, critical stage of development as professionals and global citizens responsible to the people around us."

CHAPTER 8

Thinking Strategically

Give me a place to stand, and a lever long enough, and I will move the world.

— Archimedes

Nonprofits provide crucial services caring for people in need, animals, and our environment. They step in where there are problems, and take action to alleviate hardships. One of the dangers of nonprofits is they can get caught up in providing help without their leaders taking the time to think about making the game-changing moves to solve the problem entirely, or to open up new alternatives for addressing it.

A *theory of change* is a strategy employed to solve a problem that's part of a nonprofit's mission. More specifically, what can the nonprofit do to alter the situation so the problem diminishes and, ultimately, disappears entirely? The theory of change describes what will be different as a result of a nonprofit's efforts. It's not just about the metric to measure but also about the means to achieve the desired change. This is a challenging big-picture strategic question and, especially if you're new to a cause, will require some research.

Theory-of-Change Templates

As you study the approaches of various organizations in the sector that addresses the cause you care about, see how clearly they articulate their theory of change, and whether you believe it will be effective. When you find an organization with a convincing theory of change, you can join its efforts by working with it or creating a local affiliate if it doesn't have operations in your area. As you learn more about a particular cause and its underlying problems, you may wish to become a change maker yourself. To spark some ideas, the following list provides general frameworks for making a difference in a more strategic way. You'll need to customize these templates to your specific cause. You're likely to find a number of variations of these ideas being pursued already, and volunteering to accelerate them is a great way to make a difference.

As you think about your specific problem, consider how you can apply the following change templates. Each is described in its own section following this list.

❖ Sharing best practices
❖ Reducing scope of problem at its source
❖ Building awareness to attract support
❖ Offering new alternatives
❖ Effecting change in legislation or policy
❖ Increasing demand for available assets
❖ Educating and building capacity
❖ Developing partnerships
❖ Creating new solutions

Sharing Best Practices

All too often, when someone comes up with a good idea, it doesn't have the impact it could because the people who might be receptive to it don't hear about it. The idea could be a simple one, such as "Cover your cough inside your elbow, not your hand." Unless people hear about it, and put it into practice, the benefits are limited.

Where do better ideas come from? Most often they come from someone who has already encountered the same problem, has lived in those circumstances, in that same community, and solved that particular problem with the resources at hand locally. Looking for, and spreading, local solutions is a good first step. If there isn't a local solution, perhaps there might be other communities that have faced similar issues with similar resources and have a solution you can transplant from one place to another. Along the way, some translation may be needed. Some potential solutions may literally need to be translated from French to Spanish, or from Tagalog to English; other "translations" are more abstract. In one case, there may be widespread use of cellphones for Internet access and information distribution; in another case, radio programs might be the best way to distribute the information. A baseball league that builds sportsmanship and teamwork might be more effective as a soccer league in a different state. If there isn't a real-world solution readily available, check for relevant research emerging from university or government labs. Bridging a technology or solution from the lab into the field is always challenging, as you discover the assumptions don't always hold in the real world, or find that people are set in their familiar ways and prefer not to change.

Reducing Scope of Problem at Its Source

Many ongoing relief efforts struggle to maintain their vitality and funding as they address chronic problems. Providing food and housing to those who couldn't otherwise afford it, caring for the steady stream of new arrivals at an animal shelter, or cleaning up the litter that dots our roadways and parks are all examples of important, ongoing commitments that resist easy solutions. While it's critical to provide these needed services, it's precisely such cases where we need to look upstream to see how we can reduce the need for the service. Can job-training programs help more people make it on their own? Will a program of spaying and neutering reduce the number of animals entering the shelter? Would a cash deposit on cans and bottles or aggressive enforcement of littering laws reduce the amount of roadside trash? Thinking through the causes of the specific problem you're working on can help identify high-leverage solutions that make it easier to handle the downstream problem.

Building Awareness to Attract Support

Everyone is busy, especially parents. There are so many day-to-day commitments that it's very hard to follow all the news. The structure of most reporting prevents in-depth analysis, relying instead on sound bites to capture an emotion before moving to the next story. In such a frenetic climate, it can be hard for even important issues to rise above the din. Yet broad awareness of issues is a critical first step to attracting the attention, funding, research, and advocates required for solutions to emerge. One theory of change is to transform the resources available to solve the problem by raising awareness about the issue, about the needs surrounding it, and about potential solutions, motivating a broader community to work toward bringing about the needed changes. In this way, more research, advocates, and donors are likely to emerge. You can work with traditional media, social media, or grassroots efforts. There are roles for writing, editing, publicity, and community organizing.

Offering New Alternatives

In some cases, negative outcomes such as environmental degradation or crime occur because there are no other viable choices for the people involved. Deforestation occurs in some areas because people need firewood for cooking. Introducing alternatives may enable those with limited choices to avoid these more destructive options. Examples of this theory of change include midnight basketball programs, artisan co-ops that allow handicrafts to be sold to buyers with greater appreciation (and willingness to pay) for high-quality work, and LED lights that replace hazardous kerosene lanterns.

Effecting Change in Legislation or Policy

The government is an important part of the solution for many societal problems. The government has a broad range of options to address the causes that concern you. Changing policy at a local, state, or national level can be a huge undertaking, but the results of such a change are correspondingly great. Try finding an ally in office who shares your outlook and is willing to listen to public opinion and research. Cultivate that relationship by providing timely, brief, relevant summaries of the key issues, potential solutions, and descriptions of helpful government actions. There's strength in numbers. By finding others who share your views and are willing to add their name to petitions or join you for meetings with local politicians, you'll be more likely to have your desired impact.

Increasing Demand for Available Assets

We often think of challenges from a mindset of scarcity. For example, there's not enough time, money, clean water, or affordable childcare. Finding more of the scarce good then becomes a challenge, with the search for donors or foundations who will pay for it. This theory of change encourages you to flip the standard view on its head. What do you have an excess of? How can you make that more valuable? If you're running a class training unemployed youth in graphic design, you can turn their learning experience into a pool of new logo designs for local businesses. The Adopt-a-Highway program increases the value of a clean stretch of road by offering a branding opportunity for companies wanting to get their name in front of motorists.

Educating and Building Capacity

Another key tenet of solving problems is to help people to help themselves. Like sharing best practices, this theory of change enables people to make their own progress. *Building capacity* entails enhancing the abilities that allow people to achieve measurable and sustainable results. Rather than limiting your thinking to the specific problem at hand, are there other skills the people you're helping need, or perhaps already have, in seed form? Ask them, and listen to their responses. What inhibits their effectiveness? What new skills could they learn to make them more effective?

Developing Partnerships

Wouldn't it be great if you could get more people involved in solving your problems? Perhaps there are other organizations you or the organization you're supporting could partner with to deliver your service more effectively. If you have local relationships with the soup kitchens, and they have strength in a national fundraising campaign online, working together creates a stronger team helping more people. Such alliances can make all the difference.

Education Doesn't Stop at the Classroom Door

Dr. Harry Hartzell, a retired pediatrician, is especially interested in the education young people get outside the classroom. As the advisor to a Medical Explorer post, he helps high school students learn what it's like to be a doctor, exposing them to a career he loved. The students running the Explorer post also get experience in leadership. He describes the most educational week of his own life when students from his Wilmington Friends School in Delaware visited Philadelphia, joined by students from Baltimore and Brooklyn. They lived in a Baptist church while they performed community service and toured public institutions not part of his middle-class upbringing: an insane asylum, a prison, the courts, and a sweatshop.

The educational role of nonprofits isn't limited to children, Hartzell realizes. They can also expand adults' horizons. He served on the board of Abilities United (www.abilitiesunited.org), providing services and support for people with developmental or physical challenges in Palo Alto, California. It was important to raise the organization's visibility within the community, and create interest beyond those with personal family experience of disabilities. Abilities United could provide an educational role, showing different challenges for people with disabilities, and how services can make a difference. The most effective approach was taking people on tours so they could see programs in action, and put a human face on something previously distant. "They [the visitors] go to the nursery and see kids who can't speak or walk playing with other children, following directions, and maximizing their development potential," says Dr. Hartzell. Gaining community support was vital as government support waned, now providing less than half the budget, down from 80 percent. Rather than be demoralized by the slashed funding, Hartzell (then president of the board) succeeded in leading Abilities United through a transformation. By building on their strengths, and earning income from their services, the organization overcame a feeling of dependency and victimhood, becoming a much healthier organization.

Creating New Solutions

This last theory of change requires even more creativity. When you've truly immersed yourself in a problem, you may be able to see a way to create better solutions than the current ones. Your solution could be something scientific, or an innovation in the business model used to deliver a service. Maybe you have a new way to bundle products that would be more useful, or a novel way for payments to be made on installments, making something essential more accessible to more people. Keeping your eyes open and talking to people who are most familiar with the issues may spark new ideas. Share your ideas to see if there are others who can build on or improve them. Think about low-cost ways to try out your idea, and see if it works as expected.

Choosing Your Theory of Change

Without concentrated effort, the change we desire in the world is unlikely to happen. Without an effective theory of change, though, even substantial effort can dissipate, making no lasting impact. To maximize your chance of success, think clearly about the goal and what approach you'll use to reach it. A sound theory of change can attract and direct the energies of many people working together to make a difference.

Friends of Flood Park Unite to Save Local Park

Jill Olson watched in dismay as her neighborhood's Flood Park was closed down, with state and county budgets lacking the needed maintenance and salary funds to keep it open. Her neighborhood association had a track record of organizing social occasions, and Jill thought they could come together for collective action to save the park. Her ten-year-old son Christopher helped deliver flyers announcing a neighborhood meeting with city and council officials, and more than one hundred people attended, crowding into Jill's house, occupying every possible seat including her stairs and kitchen counter. The officials listened and took notice, and created a plan to transfer ownership of the park from the county to the city. Jill and her allies, meanwhile, set up a Friends of Flood Park organization to raise money for maintenance costs and the capital improvements needed to bring the park back to life.

The Community Foundation of Silicon Valley offered to be a fiscal agent to the fledgling group, providing a way for neighbors and businesses to make tax-deductible donations. The Community Foundation also helped with budgeting and bookkeeping advice, allowing Jill to focus on her interests: communications strategy and relationship building. Ninety community volunteers came forward to clean up the park before its reopening. Their dedication won over the county officials, who agreed to reopen the park for six months while the transfer to city ownership could be analyzed and reviewed. By working together the Friends of Flood Park have won a victory for their neighborhood, and demonstrated the power of collective action.

CHAPTER 9

Implementing Your Plan

Take the first step in faith. You don't have to see the whole staircase. Just take the first step.

—Martin Luther King Jr.

We've now reached the final stage of refinement of your plan for giving back. Reviewing the results of your work so far, you have identified the cause and geography (local, national, or global) of focus, the role you'd like to play, and some thoughts about your theory of change. The next step is to learn more about your cause and the organizations addressing it. Then, you can take your preferences and ideas and find out where you can plug them in to a larger team, creating an action plan of engaging with others to assist with your cause. If this is part of a family giving plan, Listening & Learning Conversation #3 later in this chapter will enable you to create a consensus of how to proceed. After you construct a plan to fulfill your objectives, this chapter also provides some suggestions on how to approach an organization you'd like to work with, so you can be integrated into their efforts as smoothly as possible.

Researching Your Cause

During the research phase, you'll need to learn as much as you can about your cause. The key questions to answer are:

1. With whom can we join forces to work on this cause?
2. What strategies allow us to use our strengths for the biggest impact?
3. How can we educate others about this cause?

There are many potential resources to jumpstart your research. Two of the best are other people and the Internet. Other people are potentially a great source of information. Perhaps you know people with particular expertise in the causes of your interest—they might be speakers giving a talk in your town or faculty members at a local university. Have you heard of nonprofit organizations working in your field of interest with offices nearby? They might have information sessions or staff members who are willing to meet with you. In addition to the people who are already knowledgeable about the topic, it's good to talk to other people. I've been amazed how many times a friend will pass along an article on a topic of interest to me that I'd otherwise have missed. These discussions also help you formulate and deepen your own understanding of the issue. As you discuss the topic with others, you'll uncover more of your feelings about it, and seeing their reaction will help you describe the situation effectively and potentially spur others to action.

The Internet is another easy place to start your research, with access to the most comprehensive information. The websites of the organizations you've heard of are good places to start; search engines will also direct you to relevant pages.

CAUSE-ORIENTATION WORKSHEET

Cause: Protection of coral reefs	**Geography:** Global
Researcher: Steve Ketchpel	**Date:** February 2012

Shocking Facts: (synthesized from information from Coral Reef Alliance, www.coral.org)

❖ Coral reefs provide home to the ocean's greatest biodiversity, supporting an estimated one quarter of marine wildlife, one million different species of plants and animals.

❖ Reefs are threatened by climate change, with warmer water, and higher acid levels killing the coral, as well as by damage from more intense storms.

❖ Overfishing is common, threatening the fish stock, but exploitative techniques like blast fishing (using bombs to kill fish) and poison fishing (using cyanide to stun fish, making them easier to catch live, where they're sold for restaurants and aquariums) kill the coral.

❖ Some 11% of coral reefs have already been lost, with another 32% at risk in the next thirty years, if human threats aren't reduced.

❖ Coral reefs provided food and livelihood for millions of people and generate $325 billion of economic value each year.

Organizations Helping:

Coral Reef Alliance (www.coral.org); Reef Protection International (www.reefprotect.org); Coral Reef Watch NOAA (www.coralreefwatch.noaa.gov); ReefCheck (www.reefcheck.org)

Exercise: Cause Orientation and Identifying Organizations

1. To help organize your research, follow the general framework in the example on p. 95 and fill out a similar sheet with your findings about the cause you're interested in. (You can download a blank grid for this part of the exercise at www.giving-back.info.)

2. As you identify organizations that are working on your chosen cause, it's helpful to record some basic information about them, to assess whether they'd be a good partner to work with. The form below shows one sample assessment. (Again, you can download a blank grid at www.giving-back.info.) You'll want to complete a worksheet for every organization you're seriously considering as a partner in your giving-back plan.

ORGANIZATION WORKSHEET	
Organization Name	Coral Reef Alliance
Organization URL	www.coral.org
Nearest Location	351 California Street, San Francisco, CA 94104
Years working on the problem	17
Their description of the biggest challenges	Environmental change, coastal development, exploitative fishing
The solution(s) they're working on	Creating Marine Protected Areas; working with local population on sustainable management plans
Your assessment of their capabilities	Small, but effective and strategic; three five-star GreatNonprofits reviews
Published volunteer opportunities	Office work at SF office, advocate, educate, and fundraise

Next Steps

Once you've learned more about your cause and the organizations working on it, try describing it in your own words to other people. See what questions they ask, and whether you have enough information to answer them. Try balancing the facts you find with a more emotional description of the situation as well. What enrages you or pulls at your heartstrings? People often tune out news that seems too depressing. What ideas or solutions sound most promising? Can you offer an optimistic vision for changes to help your cause? As you try out different descriptions with people, notice which ones tend to lead to the most productive conversations.

As you review the organizations working on this cause, pay special attention to those that seem like a good fit. Do they have local opportunities that provide the types of roles you're interested in? Do they have a good reputation within the community? If you're considering including your family, are the organizations accustomed to having children volunteers? Would your schedule permit volunteering when they have projects? With luck, one organization will meet your needs.

If you're consulting with other family members to construct a family plan for giving, the discussion guide for Listening & Learning Conversation #3 will give you a chance to hear the research conducted by all the family members and jointly create a plan to work with a particular organization. (Feel free to skip ahead to p. 101 if you're using the book as an individual.)

Listening & Learning Conversation #3
Moving from Ideas to Action

This is where the rubber hits the road. You've chosen the causes that inspire you to give back, and you've spent time individually researching the potential opportunities for how you can come together and help, including doing the Cause-Orientation Worksheet and the Organization Worksheet earlier in this chapter. This Listening & Learning Conversation is about hearing the different proposals and choosing which ones excite your family.

Conversation Goals

1. *Listen:* Hear the research from your family members.

2. *Decide:* Decide which, if any, of the organizations and proposals you'd like to support.

3. *Set a starting time:* Set a time to start with the organization.

4. *Plan followup:* Set a time to have Listening & Learning Conversation #4, after you've started volunteering with the organization.

General Flow of Conversation

1. *Sharing findings:* All the cause researchers present their findings, starting with their "shocking facts," then moving on to their assessment in their own words, a quick review of the organizations they found working on that cause in the desired geography, and a more detailed assessment of the organization they advocate joining.

2. *Expressing appreciation:* After each cause is presented, everyone else takes a moment to express appreciation by mentioning one new thing they learned from the presentation. If there are important followup questions, they may be raised at this time as well.

3. *Reflecting and deciding:* Once all the cause presentations are complete, the reflection and decision process starts. It's best for the parents to start this phase with a summary of the research and a framework for the discussion. Here are some suggestions:

   ❖ *One proposal everyone clearly rallied around:* Build the commitment and momentum by sharing the excitement. Express appreciation for the research completed, confirm that everyone is on board, and have a yes/no vote for participation. Take the concerns of no votes seriously, and see if they can be addressed to bring everyone to a unanimous yes!

   ❖ *One strong proposal, with weaker one(s) that will be abandoned without trauma:* Start by expressing appreciation and highlighting some of the strengths of the weaker proposals, but mention the corresponding strengths of the strong proposal. Lead up to the proposal that seems to be the best, along with an appeal that by pursuing a single proposal, the family can work together and makes its greatest contribution. As you sense that consensus is reached, confirm with a vote, and close by specifically thanking those who researched other proposals but chose to go along with the winner instead.

   ❖ *One strong proposal, but weaker one(s) that won't be easily dropped:* Start by promoting the stronger proposal, including the aspects of the proposal that differentiate it from the weaker ones (though do so by describing the merits of the strong proposal, perhaps not even mentioning the weaker ones). Try to build as much excitement around the strong proposal as possible, and see if the sponsors of the weaker proposals will come around willingly. If not, decide whether you think it's feasible to pursue both plans. Describe the level of time you'll have, and resist the urge to over-commit or to make unrealistic promises for the future. If the family votes to pursue the separate proposals, do your best to provide encouragement and support, even if you don't have the time to be as helpful as you'd like to be.

❖ *No clear winning proposal, two or more that generated interest:* If there isn't enough passion behind an idea for it to be a clear win-ner, it's unlikely it will sustain the energy required to keep your family engaged over the long haul. If the spark of interest is there, and it just needs time to develop, continuing the conversation and talking more about what each person finds most interesting or compelling about the proposals may bring one to the forefront. If it doesn't, discuss frankly whether it seems as if any of the pro-posals *could* be a winner, and what more you need to understand about them. Allow the champions for the ideas additional time to prepare responses, and set up a second discussion to reevaluate the question.

❖ *No proposals that really excited people:* It's time to take a step back, and reevaluate the values and the causes that are the true mo-tivators for your family. If none of the first round of ideas captured your imagination, is it because you just weren't looking in the right place? Or perhaps you're at a stage in your lives where there's no time, and adding anything more would just be too stressful. In the first case, spend more time talking about the causes and see if there's the interest to make a second set of proposals or further develop this set. In the second case, talk about what conditions may change in the future so you have time to volunteer. Also consider whether you'd like to provide financial support instead of your time.

4. *Celebrating:* If your family has come to a final decision about which project or projects to support, it's time for a party! You've made an important joint decision, and committed to a new path that will change each of you. You've worked together as a family in what might have been a more collaborative way, learning more about all of you. Congratulations! While giving back can be a big commitment, it can

also be a lot of fun. This is a special occasion; celebrate it! As part of the celebration, try a gratitude circle: Starting with the youngest child, make that person the focus while the rest of you each say one thing that he or she said or did that you were grateful for. Move on to the next oldest until each person has been the recipient of the circle.

Special Notes for Parents

One potential risk in this Listening & Learning Conversation is if different children are researching "competing" proposals, and they feel as if you, as parents, are playing favorites among them. The best outcome is if there's a single project you can work on together as a family, in which case this conflict doesn't arise. If it does, and you can't reasonably support both proposals, be as clear as possible about the proposal-based reasons you're making your selection. Separate the proposal from the proposer, so you do not seem to be slighting one of your children, but just find the other cause more meaningful (with as specific a reason as possible). Recognize that even with your best efforts, the other child may feel hurt and need extra encouragement to find a way to get involved in and excited about the selected proposal.

A second risk is that your family overcommits. Especially in the early, enthusiastic stages, pledging five or even ten hours a week may not sound like much. Then the reality of trying to add a major commitment to your already-full calendar may hit. Perhaps the first week will work, but the second gets too busy and you feel you haven't kept your promise in the very earliest days of your efforts. While it's good to capitalize on your initial enthusiasm, it's better to set a reasonable expectation. If you've found a cause, organization, and project that are a perfect fit, you can start small and then find yourselves making more time along the way.

Special Notes for Children

After a lot of talking and research, now is the time you get to decide! You might be working on the projects you choose for a long time, so it's important to choose something that really interests you. But working on a project on your own can be hard, lonely work. So if you haven't found other family members who are willing to join in on your proposal (especially if you need a parent to volunteer with you or drive you places), see if there's another proposal that would be fun to do, even if it might not sound like it's as much fun as yours. If you're getting support for an idea you suggested, remember your family members are giving up some of their free time to give back through your idea. Thank them for it—not just now, but every time they help. Think about ways you can make it easier for them to be involved. A simple one might be to be on time and ready to go with everything you need for each of your project trips.

Reflecting on the Conversation

Take some time to write a sentence or two answering each of the following questions. This decision is an important stage of your giving-back process, and capturing how you feel now will help you see how you've changed as you look back to "the day your project started."

- ❖ What proposal did you choose?
- ❖ How do you feel about the proposal you selected?
- ❖ What was most important in causing you to choose it?
- ❖ What do you think is most exciting about the project that you're about to start?
- ❖ What's your biggest worry about the project?
- ❖ What do you hope you'll get to do as part of the project?
- ❖ What did you learn about yourself through this process?
- ❖ What did you learn about your family members through this process?
- ❖ What did people say to you in the gratitude circle that you'll remember?

Checking Out the Organization

Whether you're working on an individual or a family giving-back plan, by now you've reached a tentative decision about which organization to work with. Before you sign up for making a large gift or a long-term time commitment, it's appropriate to check that organization out thoroughly, making sure that it's a group you can trust. Although nonprofit organizations and professionals probably have a better track record than for-profit industries or politicians, there are many examples of groups that have misused their funds or failed to live up to their ideals in providing service. A good first step is to consult other people who have experience working in nonprofits to hear their assessment of the organization. If you don't have other people who can give you an informed opinion, you can do the research yourself. You can learn a lot more about an organization in the following ways:

1. Approaching the organization as a beneficiary (one who might receive services)
2. Approaching the organization as a board member
3. Approaching the organization as a donor
4. Approaching the organization as a volunteer

If you get a consistent picture of an organization managing its resources well and delivering promised services, then you've found a winner!

Approaching the Organization as a Beneficiary

Does the organization do a good job of serving the people it intends to help? The most compelling way to tell is to check it out for yourself. If you've selected a cause that's important to you because of a personal connection or you're a part of their *target market*, you're probably a well-qualified judge of the quality of its services. If not, try to find a friend who is. Then explore the public face of your organization. If your organization works with education or social services, supports the arts or legal rights, or has any service for the general public, it needs a way to attract customers. They may have a website, a 1-800 number, or drop-in sessions at their offices or a school or clinic. Check out the organization's website to see if it has the needed information presented clearly. If the organization has drop-in sessions or a 1-800 number, try those out too. Do the staff and volunteers treat you well? Are they knowledgeable? Are they the type of people you'd like to spend more time with?

In your investigation, you'll want to be respectful of the time and resources of the organization. You don't want your research to take a scarce slot away from someone who really needs the help. You can also check the organization's reviews at GreatNonprofits (www.GreatNonprofits.org), which is especially useful if the organization doesn't have offices near you or is too far removed from your experience for you to evaluate it. When you do find helpful, effective people working on a cause for which they care deeply, it will be clear and very attractive to join them.

Approaching the Organization as a Board Member

The board of directors of an organization is responsible for ensuring that the organization is achieving goals that advance its mission, and doing so as efficiently as possible. Business leaders from the for-profit world look for metrics showing how effective nonprofit efforts are, and nonprofit leaders are trained in "management by the numbers" as well. Nonprofits often claim, rightfully so, that it's very hard to track their impact and ultimate value to society. Still, savvy donors seek proof their money is being well spent, and the organizations best able to make that case with both hard numbers and heartwarming stories tend to attract the most attention and donations.

As you evaluate organizations, look at the metrics they offer. How are they measuring their success, and are they making progress over time? Don't blindly accept their metrics. Ask yourself if the metrics make sense. Organizations, like people, respond to the way they're being measured, and they may make some strange decisions if the metrics aren't properly aligned with the real mission of the organization.

As an extreme (and entirely made-up) example, imagine an organization promising to improve the self-esteem of African girls, while giving them the means to travel more easily to get to school or to do household tasks like carrying water or firewood. This hypothetical organization has amazing financial metrics: All its work is performed by volunteers, and through industry connections and a generous group of founders and officers, they spend nothing on fundraising. That is, the entire budget goes directly to programs and beneficiaries. The program staff has established a performance metric it reports faithfully: the amount of reduction in travel time for school and household tasks for the beneficiaries. The organization also measures the satisfaction of the beneficiaries with the service. Both of the metrics (improvement in transportation time and client satisfaction) are at the best possible level, and the program has no overhead, so all $10 million of their budget has gone directly into helping African girls. Sounds like a dream program worthy of your investment, right? The downside is that the fictional Sports Cars for Africa has only helped one hundred girls, giving each (delighted) beneficiary a $100,000 sports car, which gets her to school very quickly indeed.*

Obviously, this is an absurd example, but it reminds us to dig into an organization's theory of change, and make sure it matches our own intuition (or

---

* Fortunately for the girls of Africa, F. K. Day's background was in bicycles, not sports cars, so when he set up a nonprofit with the goals just described, he decided to provide bicycles (at $134 each) rather than $100,000 sports cars. More than one hundred thousand people around the world have bicycles thanks to World Bicycle Relief (www.worldbicyclerelief.org) and their corporate sponsors and donors.

convinces us why it does work, if it isn't common sense). Each of us may have a different preference, whether to provide a large amount of help to a smaller number of people or to help out a larger number of people but not as much for each. Fortunately, organizations make different choices for that tradeoff, so you're likely to find one matching your preference.

Approaching the Organization as a Donor

An effective organization needs to handle the money side well. The most important aspect is that the money it receives is spent wisely on advancing the mission of the organization. There are other necessary expenses, and an effective organization will ensure that it has the resources to keep the lights on while it pursues its mission. Living hand-to-mouth is no easier for an organization than it is for a family, and struggling to meet each payroll diverts valuable time and attention away from activities that drive the mission. On the other hand, groups that receive donor gifts and store them away for years in a rainy-day fund may not be maximizing their impact or respecting their donors' intentions.

For other tips on evaluating the fiscal responsibility of a nonprofit, see the third-party rating agencies covered in Chapter 4 and refer to Appendix A about digging into IRS 990 forms and doing the analysis yourself.

Fundraising Expenses

Looking at fundraising expenses is a common way to measure an organization's fiscal responsibility. Often, donors will have a "magic number" they look for: a threshold such as 10–15 percent, below which is acceptable, but above which is not. This is an easy way to think about fundraising. Assume an organization has a fixed budget, and if it spends more than a small fraction of that budget to raise the rest of it, then the organization isn't very efficient. To some extent, that's true. But the real situation is more complex. A very new organization may not spend much on fundraising, since its founders and board of directors will likely contribute the bulk of its early funding. As the organization seeks to expand its donor base, larger amounts will be spent on mail campaigns and online advertising, building awareness about the organization while soliciting money. When the organization becomes better known and people seek it out to make donations, the percentage spent on fundraising might drop again.

Another view, though, is to consider "the additional dollar raised." If we throw out the fixed-budget assumption, we see that the more money the organization raises, the more it has available for its programs. Imagine an organization that's distributing bags of children's books to low-income homes

Raising Funds to Save a Kenyan Nursery School

Christina Stellini had been working in international development for five years when she met Lucy, founder of St. Vincent's Nursery School & Rescue Center in Kibera, Kenya. She already had a great appreciation for the role of grassroots development organizations and knew well about the growing numbers of orphans and vulnerable children in countries hardest hit by HIV/AIDS.

Three months after meeting Lucy, Christina learned that St. Vincent's had lost its primary donor and was on the brink of shutting down. She took action immediately: first finding a partner organization in the U.S. to accept donations and get them safely to St. Vincent's, and then working to get St. Vincent's featured on Global Giving—launching a campaign that raised over $19,000 in one month through her personal network.

Christina next sought out One World Children's Fund (www.owcf.org)* and enlisted her mother and aunt to serve with her as the core fundraising group. The three visited St. Vincent's in June 2010 and have since dedicated themselves to fundraising for the organization through various events and outreach efforts. For Christina, this visit only intensified her commitment to the cause as she saw firsthand how much impact the organization has on the one hundred children served, and to the broader Kiberan community.

Christina's work kept St. Vincent's doors open during that critical time. It has also raised St. Vincent's profile in the U.S., making it easier to raise funds. In addition, she coordinates internships for St. Vincent's and has been working tirelessly to attract longer-term funding.

---

* Story used with permission of One World Children's Fund.

to encourage reading. The book bags might cost $15 each by the time they're delivered to the families. If our imaginary organization has a budget of $15,000, it can help one thousand families. Now imagine that it can spend $1,000 on a direct mail campaign to raise an additional $16,000. Its total budget is now $31,000, of which $1,000 is fundraising expense. It has $30,000 left to help two thousand families, and its percentage spent on fundraising is still a very respectable 3 percent of its budget ($1,000 out of $31,000). The executive director comes up with another idea for a fundraising event that would bring in $25,000 and cost $10,000. The $15,000 profit on the event would enable the organization to deliver one thousand more book bags. With the event, however, the fundraising expenses have climbed to $11,000 out of a $56,000 budget, or nearly 20 percent. For donors expecting to see a ratio near 10 percent, such a high fundraising-expense ratio might disqualify this organization. Yet the executive director sees the second fundraiser as a "self-funding" way of serving one thousand more families. Who's right?

I believe that the executive director is, though it's a tough call. If there were more efficient ways for the organization to raise the money, then the executive director should have done them first (or instead, if it's not possible to do both). The director should also look for ways to reduce the expense of the fundraiser (for example, find a caterer willing to make an in-kind contribution). Ultimately, if the organization ends up attracting extra support *and using the money effectively* to promote its mission, that seems more important than keeping expenses low. The picture becomes murkier, however, if this money would have been given to another organization serving the cause, and doing so more cost effectively. Partnering or merging with another organization to improve economies of scale may be the most effective way to advance the organization's underlying mission.

Approaching the Organization as a Volunteer

Nonprofit staff members are busy people, and they may see your offer to help as more of a burden than blessing. Many cold calls that organizations receive result in their having to spend more time to assess, train, and coordinate the prospective volunteers than those volunteers give back before losing interest. You can help demonstrate you're serious about your intended commitment by doing your homework first, and sending a well-written approach letter answering their key questions. If you can be introduced by someone who is already a friend to the organization, that's even better. An impressive introductory letter will answer:

- ❖ Why did you choose this cause and this organization?
- ❖ What impressed you most about the organization?
- ❖ What interactions have you had with the group so far?
- ❖ How much time do you have? When?
- ❖ What unique skills do you have?
- ❖ What would you most like to do to help? Are there specific people or projects that sound most intriguing? (You may not get your first choice, or be able to work directly with the person whose biography you saw on the website, but these expressions of interest will help them match you up.)
- ❖ Who does the organization know who knows you?
- ❖ What's the best way to reach you?
- ❖ Do you intend to involve children in your volunteering? What are their ages?

Including a donation check along with your inquiry about volunteering is a sure way to be taken seriously.

A Sample Approach Letter

As if opening a time capsule, I was able to find an approach letter I wrote in 2004 to James Dailey, then the project manager for the Grameen Foundation's project developing open-source software for microfinance. Although the URL to my background and interest is no longer active, the letter itself is a good example of an approach leading to a fruitful collaboration. I volunteered hundreds of hours that year for Grameen, using my technology background to help

```
From:     Steve Ketchpel
Sent:     Friday, October 08, 2004 3:56 PM
To:       James Dailey
Subject:  MFI open-source software

Hello James,

You've been recommended to me by a couple of different people:
Peter Bladin and Robert Sassor. I'm starting a yearlong project
at Stanford, and am interested in helping MFIs to scale through
technology. From my research so far, it seems that back-office
portfolio management software is a key step to increasing the
capacity and attracting new capital (through securitization).

I've seen the moap project (though haven't had a lot of time
to dive into all the details), and it looks like it hasn't
really attracted the critical mass of developers needed to make
progress. I'd like to speak with you to see what your plans are
relative to efforts in this space.

Peter mentioned that you were going to be in Uganda for a
couple weeks, so perhaps we can schedule some time when you
return?

A brief background on the project & on me can be found at
http://www.rdvp.org/index.php?p=project_detail&id=46

If you have recommendations on people to speak with or resources
that I should review in the meantime, I'd welcome the pointers.


Steven Ketchpel, Ph.D.
Reuters Digital Vision Fellow
Stanford University
```

them write requirements documents and conduct an evaluation of software development firms.

Approach-Letter Exercise

Take the elements on the list on p. 106, review the sample letter on p. 107, and craft an approach letter to your proposed organization. See if you can find the email address or direct phone number of the volunteer coordinator or executive director of the organization. If you're ready, send your message and set events in motion for a fruitful giving-back partnership.

Starting a New Nonprofit?

Perhaps you've talked to people, done an extensive Internet search, and come up empty. It looks as though your desires for a cause, theory of change, and geography just aren't being met, or at least not by an organization you feel would be good to work with. You're excited about pursuing your idea, so starting your own organization seems the logical next step. It can't be hard to start a new charitable organization, can it?

In theory, you're right; it's not that hard. Nearly two million people have started nonprofit organizations in the United States. It doesn't cost much to do it, and you can probably do the legal work yourself, or you certainly can with assistance from an associate at a law firm.

Just because something is (relatively) easy to do doesn't mean you should necessarily do it. Starting your own nonprofit is like buying a dog: You imagine all the fun you'll have as an owner and the tricks you'll be able to teach it, and maybe you even get offers to help care for it. If all goes well, it can be a fulfilling choice, one that brings great satisfaction, but it's also a long-term commitment. If you don't have as much help as you expect, it can feel more like a burden than a joy. If careful consideration of the drawbacks of being a nonprofit founder doesn't dissuade you, see Appendix B for more information about starting one.

CHAPTER 10

Assessing
Your Progress

Energy and persistence conquer all things.

—Benjamin Franklin

With your project underway and contact established at the organization you'd like to help, it's a good idea to schedule a progress review. As with any long-term plan, such as saving for college or retirement, it's a good idea to make sure your plans are still on track and leading to the desired outcome. Getting started is a big challenge. Therefore, it's better to schedule your first checkup after you've had three or four volunteering sessions rather than waiting too long.

To assess your progress, consider your answers to the following questions.

* What have you learned about the cause since joining the organization?
* How has your volunteering made a difference to the organization and its beneficiaries?
* What new skills have you learned or what accomplishments are you proud of?
* How could your volunteering experience be improved?
* Do you feel as if the organization is making good use of your abilities?
* Overall, do you feel good about your involvement with this organization and want to continue it or do you feel a need to cut back or shift to a different way of giving back?

If you're participating with other members of your family in the volunteering efforts, the discussion guide to Listening & Learning Conversation #4 suggests how your family can share the answers. (If you're reading the book as an individual, feel free to skip ahead to p. 113.)

Listening & Learning Conversation #4 How's It Going?

The checkups about your giving-back plan are really more of a series of Listening & Learning Conversations, held every six months or so, to make sure that you're continuing to make good progress toward achieving your goals and that the goals are still relevant. Along the way, you may be surprised to see how much you've learned from your giving back, the differences in how you feel, and the way your volunteering and giving experiences have changed your family relationships as well.

Conversation Goals

1. *Assess:* Determine whether you're making adequate progress on your project plan.

2. *Adjust:* Identify changes to the strategy or project that you're pursuing.

3. *Affirm:* Note successes and ways you have grown as individuals and a family.

4. *Assess again:* Make sure that each member of the family is having a fulfilling experience in giving back.

General Flow of Conversation

1. *Reviewing:* Start with a quick recap of the proposal that you agreed to during Listening & Learning Conversation #3.

2. *Sharing:* Have each member of the family spend two to three minutes describing what he or she has done since then. If extra help would remove a barrier or enable more progress, be sure to ask for it! Close your time with your thoughts on which of the following best matches your experience:
   - ❖ Things are going great.
   - ❖ We're on the right track, but things could be better.
   - ❖ Let's stick with the original proposal, but we need to reset our expectations and/or approach.
   - ❖ We need to abandon our original proposal and try again.

3. *Assessing progress and making adjustments:* After each member of the family has had a turn, combine the individual votes into a family assessment of your progress. Is there agreement, or are one or two people feeling like things are better or worse off than the rest of you? If you have agreement that things are going great, move on to the next stage of the conversation. Otherwise, if there are one or two people who are dissatisfied with the way things are going, see if the rest of you can help provide support. If there are widespread concerns or larger issues, take the time to discuss them, and see if changes within the existing proposal (perhaps by reducing the expectations or extending the time frame) are feasible. If family members are concerned about the organization you've selected, decide whether it deserves one more chance (and set a deadline for evaluating if it has made good) or whether it's time to find an alternative organization or even an entirely different cause. If a major change is required, you'll probably want to schedule another time to have a shorter version of Listening & Learning Conversation #3, updated with what you've learned in your experience so far. Also, recognize that sometimes things will come up that need to take priority over your giving back plan. A family member or extended family member with health issues, a challenging semester in school, or moving to a different home are just a few examples of the changes you might encounter along the way.

4. *Affirming:* Take another turn around the circle with each person spending another couple minutes to describe what he or she has liked best about the giving-back experience so far, and what he or she has learned (a new skill or insight about him- or herself, the family, or the world) as a result.

5. *Expressing appreciation:* Close the discussion with the parents offering a positive change they've noticed in each of the children, and a group acknowledgment of the great work you've done and dedication you've shown.

Special Notes for Parents

Listen for signs of frustration: Are the children feeling like they're not being taken seriously by the organization? Are they wanting to do more, but not able to because of transportation or chaperoning requirements? Are you or your spouse feeling frustrated that the addition of giving back is stressing your life in other ways? Maintaining the health, sanity, and good relationships among your family is more important than unswerving commitment to the plan you made when you didn't have as much experience and information; be flexible if it's needed.

This is also a great opportunity to be a cheerleader. Support the steps your children have taken, and show them you notice and appreciate what they're doing. If you've seen their giving-back behavior influence day-to-day home life as well, be sure to highlight it. Provide encouragement where the progress is slower than your kids would like, especially if you can share stories of your own projects that took longer than expected.

If you have two or more children, it's unlikely they'll develop the same level of interest in the project. As you encourage participation and family involvement, make sure it doesn't become a source of rivalry or perceived favoritism, where a child who is less involved feels he or she is being valued less.

Special Notes for Children

Is your giving-back project a fun thing to do? Do you feel like you're helping with the cause the way you wanted? If you are, that's great! But things often don't go as smoothly as you hope they will, and this is a good time to figure out why and maybe change them. Many times, people just don't have as much time as they think they will, and so the plans take longer than they expect. If you haven't been able to spend as much time on the project as you wanted to, is it because of your school and other activities, your parents not having the time to be involved, or the organization not being able to make use of the time you're available? If it's something to do with your family, can you find a way to make some time? How about a group promise to give up a TV show in order to give back instead? If the problem is with the organization, maybe it would be better to find another one you can help. If the problem isn't time, it could be that doing things takes longer than you expect, and you need to be patient. If you're doing what you had planned in the proposal, but it just isn't as rewarding as you expected, it's all right to say that as well. It might be hard to see the difference you're making, or the work may be more difficult than you expected. Don't give up right away, but by talking about your concerns, you might be able to get help understanding the difference you're making. If the project really isn't fun, then it's a good idea to ask about changing to something else.

Reflecting on the Conversation

Take some time to think about your answers to each of the following questions, and write a couple of sentences summarizing them. It will be fun to have a history of how you felt about the project at various points along the way. By now, you'll likely be starting to see your hard work pay off. It won't always be as easy as you'd hoped, but if you keep at it, you'll see the progress over time.

- ❖ How do you feel about the project after the family discussion?
- ❖ Who in the family needs the most support to be successful in the project, and what can you do to help him or her?
- ❖ What's your biggest worry about the project?
- ❖ What did you learn about yourself by working on this project?
- ❖ What did you learn about your family by working on this project?
- ❖ What have you learned about the cause by working on this project?
- ❖ What would you like to accomplish before the next discussion?

Planning the Next Step

As you get more deeply involved in giving back and working with an organization, whether as a family or as an individual, you'll likely find some new ideas about other contributions you can make. Your review of your current involvement will shape how you handle those new opportunities. Increasing your involvement can be rewarding, but make sure you're staying within the bounds of what you can reasonably do. Avoiding burnout is critical, and if the emphasis of your involvement is to improve family togetherness, make sure the new commitments you take on aren't coming at the cost of the family togetherness you were trying to foster.

If this review cycle has been helpful, plan ahead for the next one in another four to six months. The opportunity to come together to discuss how your family is benefiting from giving back will itself be a good bonding experience, and even if you're focusing on an individual giving-back plan, it's also important to reevaluate from time to time.

From Struggling Student to Mentor

Gabriel is a high school senior at Carlmont High School in Belmont, California. He lives in East Palo Alto, and his day begins at 6:50 AM, starting a twenty-mile daily round trip by bus to his high school. He's the youngest of five brothers and hopes to be the first of his family to attend college, thanks to the mentoring he gets from a local youth group called Youth Community Service.*

Through Youth Community Service, Gabriel volunteered to direct a public service video with a message for struggling students about how to find the help they need. His message was a personal one, targeting students experiencing challenges like the ones Gabriel used to have. After working on this volunteer public service video project, Gabriel's dream is a career in filmmaking.

When Gabriel was a freshman, he received mentoring from older students in Youth Community Service. Now he volunteers as a mentor himself, helping new freshmen to learn the ropes and make good choices. His advice? "To help others, to work hard, and to explore the world, and to find a career they really like."

Gabriel took his charges to Glide Memorial Church in San Francisco to volunteer by serving meals to the homeless. The students met homeless people and heard the stories of how they had become homeless. A reflection period after the students returned home allowed them to share what they had learned and how they felt about what they had seen and done. Gabriel says he continues to learn a lot from these service experiences.

---

* Story used with permission of Youth Community Service.

CHAPTER 11

Donating Strategically

We make a living by what we get, but we make a life by what we give.

—Winston Churchill

This chapter goes into more detail on some of the finer points of financial gifts. The focus is on Benjamin Franklin's two certainties: death and taxes. Taxes aren't always the most interesting topic (no one reads the tax code for fun), but understanding the tax treatment of donations can potentially save you a lot of money, or save time and hassle for both you and your selected charity. If any topic is less pleasant than taxes, it's death, so we cover them both in this one chapter; please don't skip it!

Making Your Gift Go Further

By now you've found an organization you want to support, and you've done your research so you know that they will use your gift well. Now you look to see how much you can afford to give, and perhaps it's not as much as you'd like. Maybe there are some creative ways you can stretch the gift to have a larger impact for the organization.

Employer-Matched Gifts

Some companies—generally larger companies that have been around a while and have a track record of producing profits—often match the gifts given by their employees and, sometimes, the gifts given by retirees, or by employees' spouses. Typically there are restrictions, such as a minimum and maximum amount, and only gifts to organizations that are tax-exempt under IRS code 501(c)3 are eligible. Religious organizations are typically excluded. Most companies will match gifts dollar for dollar, though some match at two-for-one or even three-for-one rates. You can ask your employer if they match gifts (and how the organization needs to go about claiming the match if they do).

Typically the Human Relations group will have information about any matching program the company offers.

Setting Up Your Own Matching Gift

Hearing that your company might match your gift dollar for dollar sounded appealing, didn't it? This type of matching gift can also come from other people or foundations that want to encourage giving to a particular organization. Fundraising marathons for the noncommercial jazz station KCSM in the Bay Area often feature member *challenge grants*, where a donor will offer to match all the gifts received during a particular hour, encouraging others to be more generous at that time. As a donor responding to the challenge, it can be hard to tell whether your gift really does increase the amount the matching donor will give. The donor may have a fixed planned gift, which will be given in any case, with the challenge grant hours being largely a marketing ploy.

Still, setting up a challenge grant can be motivating for both the other donors and the organization. If nothing else, the challenge grant gives you a reason to contact others in your network with the opportunity to give. That trusted referral to a set of new donor prospects is a great aid to the organization. Think about how you can structure the challenge to maximize the benefit to the organization:

❖ Do you want to encourage gifts at a certain level? Only offer to match gifts of at least that level.

❖ Do you want to help the organization add new donors to their supporter base? Your match might only apply to first-time givers.

❖ Do you want to reach the largest number of people possible? Set a limit on the amount you'll match (say, the first $20 from each donor).

❖ Do you want to encourage donations from children? Offer to match $2 for every $1 they give.

❖ Do you want to encourage online giving (or recurring giving)? Offer to match only online gifts.

Be sure to constrain the program so that even if it's wildly successful you can still afford to make your promised matching gift. That might be as simple as saying that you'll match the first $20 from the first twenty people, or that the maximum total eligible for matching is $500. Decide whether you will allow the organization to offer it to any of their donors or prospects, or limit it only to people whom you specifically invite.

Giving and Taxes

The obvious tax savings from charitable contributions is the ability to deduct the amount of your gift from your income if you itemize your deductions. When you think about the size of a gift you can afford, don't forget to factor in the tax savings you'll get from the deduction. There's another way you can also reduce your tax bill: giving *appreciated securities*, that is, stocks or other investments worth more than when you bought them.

Imagine you bought one hundred shares of Apple stock on October 24, 2001, the day they launched the iPod. Nearly ten years later, on March 12, 2011, you decide to use your shares to help the relief effort for the Japanese earthquake and tsunami. You're pleased to see that the one hundred shares that you bought for about $1,000 have gone up a lot and are worth nearly $35,200 in 2011. You sell the stock, and give $35,200 to the cause. When tax day comes, you have a deduction of $35,200 for your charitable contribution, but you also have a capital gain of $34,200, which at the 2011 capital gains rate of 15 percent is more than $5,000 in tax, offsetting most of the tax benefit of your contribution. The smarter option is to give the stock directly, and let the charity sell it. That way, you don't accrue any capital gains tax liability, saving more than $5,000 in this example.

If you want to keep your holding in the company, you can repurchase an equivalent number of shares thirty-one days or more later. If the purchase occurs in under thirty-one days, the IRS counts it as a *wash sale* and considers the purchase price of the new stock the same as the old stock. In the following figure, Part A, the *gap* where you don't own the stock, must be more than thirty days. In our Apple example, if you purchased another one hundred shares on April 1, 2011 (less than thirty-one days later), they would still have the

Wash Sales of Stocks

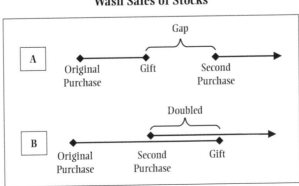

$10 cost-basis price of your original October 2001 purchase. If you'd prefer to hold the stock continuously (and you have enough available money), you can purchase an equal amount of the stock (one hundred shares, in this case), hold both lots of one hundred shares for thirty days, and on the thirty-first day sell the shares that you bought in 2001, and the more recent purchase-basis price won't reset to the old price. See Part B of the figure, where the period labeled *Doubled* is when you own both lots of shares, which must be more than thirty days.

Donor-Advised Funds

Donor-advised funds (DAFs) are a simplifying option for many midrange givers (those who make annual contributions of $5,000 or more). The accounts are offered for free by large financial institutions like Fidelity, Schwab, and Vanguard, primarily as an added service for their brokerage customers. Other, more socially motivated firms also offer DAFs, for example, the Calvert Foundation, a nonprofit socially responsible investment firm. Community foundations may also provide DAFs, giving account holders access to staff members and other resources to support their giving. Donor-advised funds function in most respects like a foundation: You establish the fund by making a contribution (of appreciated securities, for example) and then, over time, make grants from the DAF to approved charities. The main advantages offered by a DAF are:

1. Controlling the timing of the tax deduction: You're eligible for a deduction when the funds are put in the DAF, and can distribute them to charities later (though the donation is irrevocable—the money may not be taken back out of the DAF for personal use). This may be useful if you expect to have a higher taxable income one year, and wish to deduct two years' worth of donations to your nonprofits in that year, while still paying out your contributions to the organizations equally over the two years. You can also lock in your tax deduction by funding the DAF on December 30, and then have more time to assess where to make your gifts over the coming year.
2. Simplifying record keeping: All your key records for the contributions to the DAF are in one place, and likely available online. (Since you get the deduction at the time of funding the account, the individual grants to charities from the DAF aren't deductible.) Having a central location for the information also allows you to review your giving by sector or organization over time.

3. Simplifying stock gifts to small charities: As I mentioned earlier, it might save you money to give stock to an organization rather than selling it first. A smaller, local organization might not be set up to receive stock. A DAF allows you to give stock to the fund (avoiding the capital gains tax), which will sell it, and then send checks from the proceeds to the organizations you select.

4. Truly anonymous gifts when desired: Since the contribution comes from the institution that holds the DAF (like Schwab, Vanguard, or Fidelity), you can choose whether you disclose your own name as the original giver, or whether you'd prefer to keep it anonymous. In the latter case, the organization can't make a mistake and accidentally include your information in a public list, since they don't have it. It also prevents them from sending you additional solicitations or other marketing materials.

All the providers charge a base fee (an administration fee), and typically (for Fidelity, Schwab, and Vanguard) an investment fees for funds that are invested in the accounts (donations that have been made without a corresponding grant

PROPERTIES OF DONOR-ADVISED FUNDS

Provider/URL	Minimum Initial Contribution	Minimum Follow-on Contribution	Minimum Grant to Charity	Offers "Gift Cards"?	Base Fee
Calvert Foundation www.calvertgiving.org	$5,000	$250	$250	No	1%
Fidelity Investments www.charitablegift.org	$5,000	n/a	$50	Yes	0.6%
Schwab www.schwabcharitable.org	$5,000	$500	$100	No	0.6%
Silicon Valley Community Foundation www.siliconvalleycf.org	$10,000	$1,000 minimum balance	$200 in U.S., $1,000 for international organization	No	1%
Vanguard www.vanguardcharitable.org	n/a	n/a	$500	No	0.6%
YouthGive www.youthgive.org	n/a	$500 maximum	n/a	No	0%

to a nonprofit). The Calvert Foundation investment pools are exclusively socially responsible investments. The DAFs also have a $100 minimum annual administrative fee ($250 for Silicon Valley Community Foundation), as well as lower base fees for accounts that have higher balances ($500,000 and up).

A special option for youth is a donor-advised fund at YouthGive, which has no fees, no minimum, but a $500 maximum and a limited set of organizations (mostly California-based) that can receive distributions.

Making Nonfinancial Gifts

Giving unneeded toys, clothes, and household goods is a great way to make your own home less cluttered while helping others. See Chapter 6 for more on this topic. Of course, not buying as many toys, clothes, and household goods is also a way to cut down on the clutter.

Over the last few years it has become fashionable for charities to ask for donations of cars and boats. These higher-value assets can be a challenge for you to sell yourself, and the donation request is crafted to emphasize the simplicity:

Community Foundation Gives Teen an Insider's View

Andrew Olson comes from a family with a tradition of giving. His mother, Jill, worked for the United Way and the David and Lucille Packard Foundation and got a masters in communications, specializing in nonprofits. His father, Erick, worked for the American Heart Association and led a mission for a medical team to Mexico. His grandparents had also been involved in United Way, Young Life, and the American Heart Association. Andrew's parents started his giving back, by saving their change and letting Andrew decide how to give it away at the end of the year. Andrew was part of a program for teens at the Silicon Valley Social Venture Fund. The group acted as a grant maker, scheduling site visits to check out different nonprofits before ultimately selecting one to receive $5,000. His involvement inspired Andrew to become more active in his own giving. Impressed by the work of Heifer International (www.heifer.org), Andrew raised the $4,000 needed to purchase the largest gift in Heifer's catalog, an "ark" of fifteen pairs of animals: cows, sheep, oxen, camels, and water buffalo, among others. In addition to fundraising, Andrew was more excited about hands-on work, volunteering through his church youth group to repair schools and nonprofit facilities. The community foundation's program "showed the importance of the nonprofit sector to teens who are focused more on video games and friends than charity," Jill says.

"Running or not. Call us, and we'll make the arrangements to tow it away." You might be tempted by the prospect of a tax deduction of Blue Book value for that old clunker that might not be in "very good" condition. You might think of the good the organization can do with the generous gift you're offering. However, the increased visibility of this type of donation is largely because of for-profit intermediaries who handle the sales for the charity. The charity might end up with as little as 10 percent of the value, or even a flat fee as low as $45 per vehicle.*

If you still want to donate your car, it's better to find a charity that will either use the vehicle or handle the sale themselves. If the value of the car is more than $5,000, you'll need an outside appraisal. The amount of your deduction is limited to the actual sales price the charity receives for the vehicle (not the Blue Book value). If the charity intends to keep the vehicle for its own use, the Blue Book value (for the model, year, mileage, and condition) is the appropriate deduction, though it will need to be well documented.

Another common fundraiser for which your chosen organization may solicit your help is the charity auction. If your search for outgrown and unused items turned up something collectible, unique, and valuable, you may have a good auction donation. New items that don't fit your lifestyle could be candidates as well. Other auction-friendly items are use of a vacation home or sports tickets or golf-course privileges, gourmet meals prepared in the buyer's or donor's home, a novel experience with a celebrity (famous is great, but a local celebrity like a beloved art teacher can be quite a draw), or a selection of special wines. Auctioning off your professional services (as a lawyer, accountant, personal trainer, yoga teacher, or tutor) tends not to result in buyers who value your service as much as your regular clients do, so you may be better off just working extra hours and donating the proceeds of your work. Of course, the donation could make sense if you're seeking new clients or the recognition that goes along with being an auction donor. If none of these suggestions appeals to you, you may be able to secure a donation from a local business: Restaurant gift certificates, a stay at a local hotel, or museum admissions are popular items.

Estate Planning

Estate planning, legacy giving, or *planned gifts* are all more pleasant-sounding ways to talk about a topic that makes people uncomfortable: death, and what happens to your money after you die. Avoiding the topic doesn't make it go away.

---

* http://www.charitywatch.org/articles/car.html

If you don't get around to putting your affairs in order in time, it makes the probate process more confusing and expensive for everyone (else) involved. Your first concern is establishing a guardian for your minor children, if needed. Drafting a will (and keeping it up-to-date) will ensure that, in the event of your death, the people you choose will have the legal authority to care for your minor children. Your will also determines how your assets are distributed after your death. Many people choose to devote some of their estate to the charitable causes they supported during their lifetimes.

The very word *legacy* calls to mind long-term, almost larger-than-life expectations. What's your legacy? What enduring mark did you leave during your life on this planet? How will future generations remember you and your actions? Clearly, your descendants are the living part of your legacy. Their very existence is determined by the path you took through your life. Your professional achievements may be memorialized, especially creative endeavors such as a musical recording, a patent, a book, or a collection of photos. Perhaps you made a physical mark on your environment by constructing a new home or planting a garden or grove of trees. Another part of your legacy is the way you treated other people, their recollections of your relationship, and the efforts you made to improve their lives. That is, giving back can be an important part of your legacy.

Your will represents your final opportunity to influence the world. Rather than let the state decide what you would have wanted (if you die without a will), take the time to consider the legacy you'd like to leave, and work with a lawyer (if needed) to write it into a precise, legally binding document, a plan for the future beyond your lifetime. Providing for your family is probably the foremost consideration on your mind, and appropriately so. However, creating the full vision of your legacy may mean incorporating others, such as those organizations you feel are transforming the world into the fuller expression of what you envision for it. During your lifetime, you supported those organizations with your volunteer time and donations. After death, you can still provide financial support from a portion of the assets you accumulated over a lifetime.

There are three different approaches to thinking about a legacy gift.

1. As a memorial gift
2. As income replacement
3. As a bold, strategic gift

The first approach, memorial giving, is simply to include the organization in your will. A token amount shows the organization was an important part in your life, an association you want to acknowledge even on the solemn occasion of your death. Perhaps you include favored organizations as suggested recipients of memorial gifts.

A second approach to legacy giving is to think about *income replacement* for the organization. If you've been a significant donor over a period of years, will the absence of your gift cause them hardship? If you fear the answer might be yes, and you have the means to do so, you can establish an endowment-style gift that generates enough income on an annual basis to match what you gave each year during your life. The typical endowment payout policy is about 5 percent of its value (which assumes investment returns are slightly above that, to maintain the real, inflation-adjusted value of the principal). So you'd need to start with an amount that is twenty times what you'd like to give on an annual basis. For example, if you make a $1,000 gift each year to a local organization that teaches urban gardening, and wanted to sustain that gift "in perpetuity" after your death, making a $20,000 bequest would likely enable them to draw $1,000 worth of interest each year without running out of money. Of course, not every organization has the structure in place or the discipline to maintain that type of long-range planning. If you're worried your wishes for an endowment-style gift will be beyond their capabilities, you may be able to find a community foundation that has more of the financial experience and structure in place to administer the gift over the long term. Donor-advised funds may also provide the service, though that may require a $100,000 or larger initial grant.

The third approach to legacy giving is to consider a bold, strategic gift. At the time the organization receives your bequest, you won't need the money anymore. So, free from personal attachment, what would a larger gift enable the organization to do? Hire more staff? Start a new program? Remodel their facility to make it more suitable for the people they're helping? Of course, it's hard to predict today what the organization's priorities will be years from now when they receive the gift, but it's still a useful thought exercise to consider the potential impact of different gifts. Don't limit yourself to a single organization, but think about which one(s) would make the best use of your gift, or be most transformed by it.

As a final thought experiment, ask yourself the question "Why wait?" Being able to see your gift make a significant difference to a favorite organization is a powerful validation of your success. There are certainly reasons to save the assets you need for your family's long-term well-being, but if there's an opportunity that captures your imagination, think about whether it would be feasible to do both. Discuss it with your family to see if they share your enthusiasm. Sometimes a bold vision will radically change your priorities, as it did for the Salwen family, who tell their story of downsizing and giving half the proceeds of their house sale to the Hunger Project in *The Power of Half* (Salwen & Salwen, 2010).

Tips for Families with More to Give

If your family is fortunate enough to be able to give back quite a bit more than the average family, there are more options for you to consider. The process recommended in this book for determining where to give is still worthwhile: discovering your family's values, translating them into causes and organizations you can support, and choosing one or more projects in which you can take part together. As you choose how to deploy your resources, the same types of questions come up: Do you want to concentrate all your efforts within one cause and one organization, or would you rather diversify your efforts? Although it's a personal choice, you're wise to be cautious if you find an organization has become too dependent on your generosity. It can be risky for the organization, if you later decide to shift your attentions elsewhere. It can also be unhealthy for the organization if they become too eager to maintain your involvement and start to warp their mission to their perception of your interests.

The question of how much to give takes on added significance for a family with greater means. Investment manager and philanthropist Claude Rosenberg was especially concerned with helping wealthier families judge their giving capacity. In addition to writing an excellent book on the topic, *Wealthy and Wise* (Rosenberg, 1994), he often spoke on the concept of *new tithing*, where the affordability of a gift is measured compared to net worth, arguing that this principle provides a better yardstick than current income. His reasoning relies on two important insights:

1. Living expenses make up a lower percentage of income for wealthier families, even taking into account higher expenses for customary luxuries chosen by the wealthy. In his example (Rosenberg, 1994, p. 53), a household with an income of $60,000 might spend $39,000 (65 percent) on living expenses. Meanwhile, a second family with an income of $590,000 might spend $232,000 (39 percent) on living expenses. Therefore, the wealthier family has a greater surplus not just on an absolute basis, but on a relative basis as well.

2. The availability of earning (financial) assets tends to act as an accelerator. The earnings (interest and dividends) tend to be added on top of an income that was already sufficient to cover expenses, and therefore go straight into added savings, increasing the earning assets for the following year.

Among several other examples, Rosenberg follows a hypothetical taxpayer who earns $1.86 million per year and has investable assets of $16 million. Following a number of assumptions the financial manager Rosenberg considers conservative, he shows the person could make annual gifts of $900,000 (almost 50 percent of annual income) and *still* expect to increase his or her net worth. While not many of us share the resources of his example, Rosenberg makes a good point when he says, "*Money is money, it knows not its source, and it knows not the difference between a dollar of leftover income and a dollar representing an Earning Asset.*"* For those with a financial bent or with a higher level of assets, Rosenberg's book offers a specific methodology to determine the affordability of ongoing giving at a particular level measured against income and net worth. For a gentler introduction for those with an interest in gaining familiarity without all the financial detail, see the article that Rosenberg coauthored with Tim Stone in the Fall 2006 issue of the *Stanford Social Innovation Review* (Rosenberg & Stone, 2006). Unfortunately, the online calculator described in the article is no longer available with the dissolution of the New Tithing Foundation following Rosenberg's death.

In addition to where to give, and how much to give, families with greater wealth have the added question of whether to use a different *vehicle* (tax entity) for their giving.

Family Foundations

One option open to families with more significant means is that of creating a *family foundation*. A family foundation is similar to a donor-advised fund, except that where the DAF gives you the illusion of control, with a family foundation you really do have control. In a DAF, the financial institution holding the funds has the ultimate authority to approve or deny the donors' suggested grants. In practice, they don't deny grants that fall within IRS guidelines, but they could. A family foundation can ensure that all desired grants are made, and can also hire employees to handle research and administration, for example. Of course, the overhead of an employee only makes sense for families

---

* *Wealthy and Wise*, p. 67. The italics are Rosenberg's.

making hundreds of thousands of dollars of grants each year. *Building Family Unity through Giving* (Stone, 2008) is a useful resource that describes the experiences of the Graham family in setting up and running a family foundation with a multigenerational board.

Community Foundations

It's precisely the increased economies of scale that *community foundations* offer as their advantage. Community foundations offer the financial structure and staff to support the giving practices of their donors, who typically live in the same geographical area. Depending on the asset and giving level of the donor, the community foundation may offer a DAF or a *supporting organization*, which is a separate entity with its own taxpayer ID and board (though probably controlled by community-foundation members). The donors and community-foundation staff collaborate on grant-making and investment decisions. The Silicon Valley Community Foundation publishes a nice summary of the tradeoffs between a donor-advised fund, a supporting organization, and a private foundation.[*]

---

[*] http://www.siliconvalleycf.org/docs/giving/svcf-how-to-give-options-chart.pdf

CHAPTER 12

Conclusion

You give but little when you give of your possessions.
It is when you give of yourself that you truly give.

—Kahlil Gibran

Congratulations! I hope that you're well along the path to giving back in a way you find meaningful. Through reading, thinking about, and discussing this book with your family and others, you may have realized there are plenty of ways you can get involved with giving back. It's not possible for you to do everything, and it's probably best not to even think about trying. Focus on the things that are most meaningful to you and your family. Focus on the areas where you can make a unique contribution: causes that draw on your strengths and that you feel good about sharing with your friends and wider network. Notice how you're feeling over time, and see how your involvement changes. Have fellow volunteers become friends? Have you looked for other ways to volunteer with this group or with others? Have you developed new skills or accomplished projects that looked daunting when you started? Have you learned more about your family and seen changes in them as they get involved? Have you become more aware of the news and issues surrounding your cause and interest?

The choices you've made to give back will transform your life in ways great and small. You'll meet new people you might never have gotten to know otherwise; you may think differently about the way you spend your money and plan for your future. You may learn new skills and redefine what you consider to be success.

Your skills, time, and money empower you to make a difference in the world. By thinking critically about how you will use that power, you can be confident that your choices reflect your most important values and lead to projects with the potential to bring about a world closer to your ideal.

It's an exciting journey, and a lifelong one. I hope that you find fulfillment as you navigate it!

Understanding the IRS 990

Evaluating the trustworthiness of a nonprofit organization is challenging. How they handle their money is often a reflection of how they handle other aspects of their operations. Several nonprofit rating agencies offer an analysis summarized by a simple star rating (see Chapter 4), but to evaluate an organization that isn't rated, or to dig deeper into one that is, you can typically find the basic financial information online.

Almost all nonprofit organizations (except religious organizations) are required to file an annual form with the IRS called the 990. The completed 990 forms are available to the public through third-party websites like Charity Navigator (www.charitynavigator.org) and GuideStar (www.guidestar.org). They typically maintain the last four or five years' worth of forms. The key elements of the form show the amount and source of income, the level of assets, and the usage of funds, with a focus on highlighting some areas that might be warning signs for donors, such as money spent on salaries, fundraising, or consultants. Like individual tax returns, there's a short-form 990 EZ that smaller organizations may be able to file. Even the short form is several pages long, with at least the complexity of a personal income-tax form.

Here are some of the key questions that a 990 can help you answer:[*]

1. Is the organization financially viable?
   ❖ What were its revenue and expenses?
   ❖ What are its asset levels?
   ❖ How large is its endowment?
   ❖ How have the numbers been changing over the last few years?

---

[*] The California Attorney General's Office has put together a very nice pamphlet: "A Donor's Guide to IRS Form 990" as part of "Guide to Charitable Giving for Donors" at http://ag.ca.gov/charities/publications/CharitiesSolicitation.pdf.

2. Is the organization efficient?
   ❖ How much does it spend on fundraising?
   ❖ How much does it spend on management?
   ❖ Is it spending the money that it raises or just investing it?

3. Is there any evidence of impropriety in the financial operations or governance?
   ❖ Are the levels of compensation for employees and directors reasonable?
   ❖ Are the payments to contractors reasonable?
   ❖ Are there any *insider transactions* with officers?
   ❖ How many directors are there, and how much time are they spending on the organization?
   ❖ Is the organization truly publicly supported, or is there a behind-the-scenes concentration of wealth and support?

A key weakness of the 990 form for evaluating a nonprofit is that it focuses only on the money, not on the outcomes achieved. As such, it's only one piece of the due-diligence work to decide whether an organization is worthy of investment.

If you're interested in an in-depth analysis of one organization's IRS 990 form as a guidepost for your own evaluations of organizations you're considering supporting, visit my website at www.giving-back.info, where you'll find a detailed look at the specific line items on the 990 form of Doctors Without Borders (also known by their French name *Médecins Sans Frontières*, or MSF) as an example.[*]

---

[*] Aside from a small memorial gift, I don't have any specific tie to this organization, and I did my analysis entirely from the publicly available 990 information, without additional input or review by Doctors Without Borders.

Starting Your Own Nonprofit

When you're excited about advancing a cause you care about, you might find it tempting to create a new organization to administer the project, collect donations, and recruit volunteers. While setting up a new organization isn't particularly hard or expensive, it does saddle you with a long-term commitment, and may take away time and energy from working directly on your cause. If you can pursue your plan, at least the initial stages of it, before formalizing your operations with an official organization, you're wise to do so. You can ensure that your project will be a sustaining interest, and that you truly have the necessary skills to lead, recruit, and fund the operation before getting too deeply committed.

Before you start your own nonprofit organization, here are some things to consider.

1. Check twice to make sure there isn't an existing group already doing what you propose.
2. Review your own prior commitments and leadership experience. Do you have experience leading organizations through challenges for years at a stretch? Do you lose interest and move on to the next thing when you run into hardship? Check with your spouse, close coworkers, or good friends, who can also vouch for your ability to stick with it when things get hard.
3. Consider the alternatives: Is there a way around setting up another organization? You may be taking on a significant amount of new work that isn't really necessary. For example:
   ❖ Could you do the work without an official organization? If you don't need to receive tax-deductible donations to run your operations, you may not need a formal organization at all.

❖ Could you locate a fiscal agent to act as a sponsor for your organization, receiving your donations but letting you operate as a largely independent entity?

❖ Could you offer to start your program within an existing organization?

If starting a new organization still seems the best way to proceed, I recommend starting two different tasks in parallel:

1. Start doing the work your organization will do. Make sure you can do the work (or at least as close to the real work as possible), make sure that you enjoy it, and make sure that it's truly helpful to the intended beneficiaries.

2. Start developing the legal, financial, and human resources you need for the new organization.

   a. Clearly articulate what you plan to do, and how you'll be different from existing agencies.

   b. Test out your message on prospective volunteers, donors, and beneficiaries. Do other people get as excited as you are? Do the prospective beneficiaries agree that the service is needed? Are there other people who will help you fund and run the organization?

   c. Find other people who will serve as officers and directors for your organization. Together, they should be willing to commit to giving a significant amount (for example, $3,000 per year) for the basic operating expenses, as well as participating in fundraising at the goal level you'll need to carry out your plans.

   d. Find an attorney and a CPA who can help you set up the organization and submit the needed forms (like the 990) to the government. Ideally, these professional service providers are so convinced about the cause and potential for this new organization that they agree to work *pro bono*, without charging you for their time, though you'll still need to pay filing fees. Nolo Press publishes a great do-it-yourself guide to incorporating a nonprofit (Mancuso, *How to Form a Nonprofit Corporation*, 2011) with a special version for California residents (Mancuso, *How to Form a Nonprofit Corporation in California*, 2011). Nolo Press also offers a useful tax guide for nonprofits (Fishman, 2010), among other resources.

Internet Resources

The following list includes the websites mentioned elsewhere in the text. For your convenience, at my website (www.giving-back.info) you'll also find the links to all these resources (and can click on the live links rather than having to type the addresses).

Volunteer Opportunities

All for Good (**www.allforgood.org**) includes the listings from several other sites, and so appears to be the most comprehensive. It offers the ability to restrict the search by geography, cause area, and date range, and so is a good place to start.

VolunteerMatch (**www.volunteermatch.org**) is another nationwide site. The advanced-search tab allows restricting the results to those opportunities good for kids, teens, or groups. Although you can't easily filter the results to the date(s) you're interested in, you can sort by date.

HandsOn Network (**www.handsonnetwork.org**), with 250 "action centers," lists many opportunities and has quite a bit of helpful information.

Evaluating Nonprofits

GreatNonprofits (**www.GreatNonprofits.org**) compiles reviews from volunteers and donors about each organization. In addition to a star rating system, they evaluate the strengths and opportunities for improvement.

Charity Navigator (**www.charitynavigator.org**), focuses on more thorough analyses of larger organizations. In addition to the financial metrics from the IRS 990 forms, a second dimension of "transparency and accountability" is measured with objective factors such as the posting of a privacy policy. A star rating system tracks the organizational effectiveness and efficiency. GreatNonprofits' reviews of the organizations are available here as well, along with user comments. They have indicated future plans to evaluate the impact of organizations.

GuideStar (www.guidestar.com) offers free access to recent IRS 990 forms and GreatNonprofits' user reviews. A subsidiary of GuideStar, Philanthropedia (www.myphilanthropedia.org) has consulted experts to evaluate the most promising nonprofits in about twenty different program areas. Although the coverage of organizations is limited (to about four hundred organizations), these are considered the best as selected and reviewed by more than two thousand experts from the field. Each organization has a brief summary of the results achieved as well as a one-sentence summary of strengths and weaknesses from about twenty experts, categorized into higher-level themes.

The Better Business Bureau (www.give.org) conducts a free evaluation of applications made by nonprofits. Those that pass a series of twenty standards of charity accountability are awarded a seal. You can also file a complaint about a charity on this site.

GiveWell (www.givewell.org) does its own thorough evaluation of the impact of organization's programs (as presented by the organization) as well as of the finances. It recommends only 2 percent of the organizations considered.

American Institute of Philanthropy (www.charitywatch.org) rates about five hundred organizations by the percentage of funds that goes to program expenses and the fundraising cost to bring in public donations, among other criteria.

Wiser.org (www.wiser.org) is a network of people and organizations with a sustainability focus. Users can submit comments about organizations. WiserGiving.org is a companion site that offers a quiz to determine your giving style, and will be releasing more features to help individuals with their giving strategy.

Volunteering Vacations and Gap-Year Assignments

Volunteer Guide (www.volunteerguide.org) does a nice job of offering a selection of different organizations within each cause and approach.

Abroad Reviews (www.abroadreviews.com) offers reviews from past travelers. They have dozens of candid reviews for the most prominent organizations, some of which warn you away because of issues of safety, organization, or inflated cost.

The International Volunteer Programs Association (www.VolunteerInternational.org) is a portal site that allows you to search by region, country, cause, and duration.

Gift Cards for Donations

Kiva (www.kiva.org) provides microcredit loans to borrowers around the world to start or expand their businesses.

DonorsChoose (www.donorschoose.org) lists classroom projects submitted by teachers that advance education in the United States.

GlobalGiving (www.globalgiving.org) enables donors to choose from hundreds of qualified projects across a range of causes around the world.

Network for Good (www.networkforgood.org) lists more than a million nonprofits that can receive donations through their *Good Card*.

Companies Offering Donor-Advised Funds

Calvert Foundation (www.calvertgiving.org) requires a minimum contribution of $5,000.

Fidelity Investments (www.charitablegift.org) requires a minimum initial contribution of $5,000, and makes grants in $50 increments.

Charles Schwab (www.schwabcharitable.org) requires a minimum initial contribution of $5,000, and makes grants in $100 increments.

Silicon Valley Community Foundation (www.siliconvalleycf.org) requires a minimum initial contribution of $10,000, and makes grants with a $200 minimum (domestic) or $1,000 (international).

Vanguard (www.vanguardcharitable.org) doesn't specify a minimum initial contribution, and makes grants in $500 increments.

YouthGive (www.youthgive.org) is a "starter" donor-advised fund intended for youth. It has no fees and no minimum investment (but a $500 maximum) and a manageable set of recipient organizations described in a youth-friendly way.

Birthday Gifts for a Cause

Clover by Clover (www.cloverbyclover.com) provides the structure for a child to set up a party/cause page, designate an organization to receive a percentage of the gifts, and potentially retain a percentage for him- or herself to purchase a "single special gift." The administrative fee of 10 percent, however, cuts into the gift amount.

Jolkona Foundation (www.jolkona.org) isn't quite as kid-friendly, but it does send 100 percent of gifts received to the designated cause.

Reports, Statistics, and Other Resources

http://ag.ca.gov/charities/publications/CharitiesSolicitation.pdf
Harris, K. D. California State Attorney General prepared "Guide to Charitable Giving for Donors." Contains an excellent description of reviewing the IRS 990 form.

http://dunn.psych.ubc.ca/files/2010/12/If-Money-Doesnt-make-you-happy.Nov-12-20101.pdf
Dunn, E. W., Gilbert, D. T., & Wilson, T. D. (2010, December). "Research White Paper: If Money Doesn't Make You Happy, Then You Probably Aren't Spending It Right."

http://psychcentral.com/lib/2007/how-children-develop-empathy
Kutner, L. (2007). How Children Develop Empathy. *Psych Central.*

http://scienceblogs.com/notrocketscience/2008/08/children_learn_to_share_by_age_78.php
Blog entry by Ed Yong summarizing *Nature* journal article on experiments in children's sharing.

http://www.americorps.gov
Information site, complete with videos and application forms, for people considering serving with the United States AmeriCorps programs, including VISTA.

http://www.bea.gov/national/txt/dpga.txt
2011 U.S. Bureau of Economic Analysis: Statistics including aggregate personal income. Accessed on July 7, 2012.

http://www.boardsource.org/Knowledge.asp?ID=3.368
BoardSource Q&A: "Ten Basic Responsibilities of Nonprofit Boards."

http://www.boldergiving.org/
Bolder Giving tells the stories of real people who have made very generous gifts, and provides tools to help you think and talk about your giving. Back issues of *More than Money* are available here.

http://www.catchafire.org
Volunteer projects requiring professional skills like brand identity, web development, finance, or public relations are described here. Nearly all are in New York or Boston, though the service could scale nationally (and some projects don't require you to be onsite).

http://www.charitywatch.org/articles/car.html
American Institute of Philanthropy's article "Tips for Donating a Car to Charity."

http://www.dosomething.org
A website for teens interested in starting their own clubs or projects. Information resources as well as videos and past project write-ups. Do Something also provides grants up to $500.

http://www2.guidestar.org/organizations/13-3433452/doctors-without-borders-usa.aspx
GuideStar's information page about Doctors Without Borders (from which their IRS 990 may be downloaded).

http://www.loanback.com/
A commercial website that helps create clear, binding personal loans.

http://www.mifos.org/
The Microfinance Open Source project launched by Grameen Foundation, in production with about twenty institutions providing loans to more than 250,000 people, now supported by an open-source community.

http://www.nolo.com/legal-encyclopedia/promissory-notes-personal-loans-family-30118.html
Nolo Press article on making personal loans, with pointers to their forms.

http://www.peacecorps.gov
Information site, complete with videos and application forms, for people considering serving with the United States Peace Corps.

http://www.philanthropy.iupui.edu/news/2012/06/pr-GivingUSA 2012.aspx
Press release offering highlights of the 2011 edition of this oft-cited annual survey on giving statistics.

http://www.serve.gov/toolkits.asp
A collection of how-to guides from United We Serve to organize your own project. The website offers a range of other resources as well. Its listings of volunteer opportunities are provided by All for Good.

http://www.siliconvalleycf.org/docs/giving/svcf-how-to-give-options-chart.pdf
Silicon Valley Community Foundation's comparison chart of donor-advised funds, supporting organizations, and private/family foundations.

http://www.ssireview.org/articles/entry/a_new_take_on_tithing
Authors Claude Rosenberg and Tim Stone describe how donors, especially those with greater means, can afford to give more than the traditional tithe.

Bibliography

Arrillaga-Andreessen, L. (2012). *Giving 2.0: Transform Your Giving and Our World*. San Francisco: Jossey-Bass.

Boles, N. B. (2009). *How to Be an Everyday Philanthropist*. New York: Workman Publishing.

Bolles, R. N. (2011). *What Color Is Your Parachute?* (2011 ed.). Berkeley, CA: Ten Speed Press.

Corporation for National and Community Service, Office of Research and Policy Development (2007). *The Health Benefits of Volunteering: A Review of Recent Research*. Washington, DC.

Fehr, E., Bernhard, H., & Rockenbach, B. (2008). "Egalitarianism in Young Children," *Nature*, 1079–1083.

Fishman, S. (2010). *Every Nonprofit's Tax Guide* (1st ed.). D. Fitzpatrick, Ed. Berkeley, CA: Nolo Press.

Friedman, J. (2003). *The Busy Family's Guide to Volunteering*. Beltsville, MD: Robins Lane Press.

Gary, T., & Adess, N. (2008). *Inspired Philanthropy* (3rd ed.). San Francisco, CA: Jossey-Bass.

GreatNonprofits.org (2009). *Great°Guide to Giving and Volunteering*. P. Ni, & D. Weir, Eds. San Francisco, CA: GreatNonprofits.org.

Hanks, L. (2009). *The Mom's Guide to Wills and Estate Planning*. Berkeley, CA: Nolo Press.

Kielburger, C., Kielburger, M., & Page, S. (2010). *The World Needs Your Kid: Raising Children Who Care and Contribute*. Vancouver, BC, Canada: Greystone Books.

Kinder, G. (1999). *Seven Stages of Money Maturity*. New York: Dell Publishing.

LeMay, K. (2009). *The Generosity Plan*. New York: Atria Books/Beyond Words.

Levinson, D. T. (2010). *Everyone Helps, Everyone Wins*. New York: Plume.

Lewis, B. A. (2008). *The Teen Guide to Global Action*. Minneapolis: Free Spirit Publishing.

Loeb, P. R. (2010). *Soul of a Citizen* (rev. 2010 ed.). New York: St. Martins Press.

Mancuso, A. (2011). *How to Form a Nonprofit Corporation* (10th ed.). J. Lee, Ed. Berkeley, CA: Nolo Press.

Mancuso, A. (2011). *How to Form a Nonprofit Corporation in California* (14th ed.). Berkeley, CA: Nolo Press.

McKay, M., Forsyth, J. P., & Eifert, G. H. (2010). *Your Life on Purpose*. Oakland, CA: New Harbinger Publications.

Menzel, P., & D'Aluisio, F. (2008). *What the World Eats*. Berkeley, CA: Ten Speed Press.

Morris, A., & Heyman, K. (1992). *Houses and Homes (Around the World Series)*. New York: Lothrop, Lee & Shepard Books.

Post, S. G. (2011, December). *It's Good to Be Good: 2011 Fifth Annual Scientific Report on Health, Happiness and Helping Others*. Retrieved February 11, 2012, from International Journal of Person Centered Medicine: http://www.ijpcm.org/index.php/IJPCM/article/view/154 or http://unlimited loveinstitute.com/publications/pdf/Good_to_be_Good_2011.pdf.

Price, S. C. (2001). *The Giving Family*. Washington, DC: Council on Foundations.

Rosenberg, C. (1994). *Wealthy and Wise*. Boston: Little, Brown.

Rosenberg, C., & Stone, T. (2006). "A New Take on Tithing," *Stanford Social Innovation Review*, Fall edition.

Sabin, E. (2004). *The Giving Book*. New York: Watering Can Press.

Salwen, K., & Salwen, H. (2010). *The Power of Half*. New York: Houghton Mifflin Harcourt Publishing.

Smith, D. J. (2011). *If the World Were a Village* (2nd ed.). Toronto, Ontario, Canada: Kids Can Press.

Somerville, B., & Setterberg, F. (2008). *Grassroots Philanthropy*. Berkeley, CA: Heyday Books.

Stone, D. (2008). *Building Family Unity through Giving*. San Francisco: Whitman Institute.

Tierney, T. J., & Fleishman, J. L. (2011). *Give Smart*. New York: PublicAffairs.

Twist, L., & Barker, T. (2003). *The Soul of Money: Transforming Your Relationship with Money and Life*. New York: W. W. Norton.

United Nations Volunteers (2011). *State of the World's Volunteerism Report*. Denmark: United Nations Volunteers.

Weisman, C. (2006). *Raising Charitable Children*. St. Louis: F. E. Robbins & Sons Press.

Acknowledgments

This book is the product of many conversations and the generous feedback of many people who read drafts and offered their suggestions for improvement. As I mentioned in the Preface, formative examples of giving in my life included my parents, Pat and Paul Ketchpel, as well as the Boy Scouts and the churches I grew up in. The ministers of those churches, including the United Campus Christian Ministry at Stanford, deserve special mention, notably Revs. Lyman Potter, Bob Naylor, Clyde Dodder, Sandra Hulse, David Howell, Jim Burklo, Elena Larssen, Eileen Altman, Daniel Ross-Jones, and Geoff Browning.

The two people who had the largest impact as formal teachers of philanthropy were Laura Arrillaga-Andreessen and Mark Moulton, and I was lucky to be surrounded by truly giving people whose actions offered the lessons that I and others studied. Deserving of special mention here are Dave Ahn, Marie Baylon, Margaret Beeler, John Binkley, David and Sally Brown, Marilyn Burnes, Sally Campbell, Scott Carey, Ruth Carleton, Ray Casavant, Fred and Imogene Chancellor, Maureen Chandler, Alex Counts, Mike and Susan Davis, Andy Dimock, Leif Erickson, Megan Swezey Fogarty, Anne Galli, Hector Garcia-Molina, Dick and Joan van Gelder, Diana Gibson, Bob Graham, Norma Grench, Sean Hansen, Elizabeth Hansot, Harry and Susan Hartzell, Elinor Heath, Bing and Jennie Heckman, Jim Hewlett, Cedric and Juli Hughes, Kenneth Hughes, Lynn and Marilyn Hunwick, Cecil Lamb, Rob and Lucinda Lenicheck, Anne Loftis, Melissa Anderson and Howard Look, Debby and Tom Martin, Derek Mayweather, Marty Miller, Stina Miller, David and Lynn Mitchell, Jim Peters, Daryce Peterson, Marilyn and Blake Putney, Margarita Quihuis, Anna and Frank Rehwinkel, Bill and Carolyn Reller, Ben and Judy Roberts, Dick and Gerrie Roe, Jean Roth, Barbara Slone, Don Skipwith, Grant Sontag, Russ and Sheila Stevens, Alan and Carole Stivers, Samina Sundas, Cammy and Einar Sunde, Ann Swanberg and Chris Miller, Jim Swanson, Nan Swanson, Anne Wilson, Hans and Elizabeth Wolf, Greg Wolff and Sunita de Tourreil, Sue Ann Yarbrough, Anna and David Yee, and Lavinia Yee. All have given of themselves to make our community, nation, and world a better place to live.

Many people helped with the book, by reading drafts, providing introductions to people with inspiring stories (or their own), giving advice on the nitty-gritty process of writing a book, or offering encouragement along the way. Special thanks to Karen Andre, Jose Arocha, W. Ross (Bill) Ayers, Sam Bajaj, Archan Basu, Dipak Basu, Chloé Blanchard, Dick and Marci Bolles, Robert Bosch and Ming Tsai, Liz Bremner, Tarra Christoff, Amy Cleary, Dan Clifford, Kate Cochran, Alexa Culwell, Zeina Daoud, Hill and Don Dewey, Randy and Debbie Dewey, Sarah Diego, Alan Drummer, Chris Dudley, Peggy Duvette, Lluvia Esparza, Eve Evangelista, Naomi Friebert, Amit Garg, Anil Godhwani, Gautam Godhwani, Brian Goler, Justin Gordon, Linda Grossman, Amy Snyder Hale, Liza Hanks, Tracy Herrick, Sony Holland, Li Hong, Kristin Howell, Kurt Huang, Renda James, Jan Jannink, Lauren Janov, Pradeep Javangula, Eugene Kim, Jason Koenig, Sanjay Krishnaswamy, Meredith Kunz, Joe Kusnan and Jeanne Oh, Vicki Laffen, Paul Lamb, Justin Lin, Saundra and Bob Lormand, Trevor and Alice Loy, Shazia Makhdumi, Mary McBride, Rashmi Menon, David Minifie, Nikki Mirghafori, Holly Mitten, Susan Morey, Perla Ni, Jill Olson, Durga Pandey and Ruchi Bajaj, Jenny Patchen, Golda Philip, Lakshmi Reddy and Sunil Vemuri, Stan Rosenschein, Karen Routt, Terri Sarappo, Sonam Sarawgi, Peter Sass, Marina Spivak, Soma Stout, George Strong, Shirley Sun, Joe Tan, Vasuki Thangamuthu, Emily Tucker, Gail Uilkema, Jill Vialet, David Viotti, Elisa Waggoner, Helen Wang, Todd Werth, Will Whitted, Artie Wu, Cheryl Young, and Teddy Zmrhal.

Thank you also to those who provide inspiring examples of giving; whether or not there was the chance to include your inspirational story in this book, your actions have profound second-order effects as they encourage the rest of us to follow your lead.

So many people have provided me with assistance, information, and inspiration over the years that, despite my best efforts, I may not have managed to acknowledge every one of you individually; please know that your generosity has touched me deeply.

It seems fitting to close with a tip of the hat to the team of professionals who helped me produce the book. Dave Blake created the graceful design for the text, and Marites Bautista implemented it with amazing speed and accuracy. Finally, I give a bow of deep gratitude to my editor, Nancy Carleton. Her wisdom and guidance, as well as personal experience with the topic, have significantly shaped the final result. Her encouragement, patience, and flexibility made major obstacles seem less daunting.

—SPK, August 2012

About the Author

Steven Ketchpel, Ph.D., studied computer science at Harvard University and Stanford University, culminating in a Ph.D. from Stanford in 1998. His research work led to sixteen publications in the areas of e-commerce, software agents, digital libraries, and user experience. He cofounded web customer experience management company Vividence in 1998, working in various technical leadership, development, and research capacities until its acquisition by Keynote Systems in 2004. He returned to Stanford as a visiting scholar in the Reuters Digital Vision Program, collaborating for a year with the Grameen Foundation's Technology Center on the development of the Mifos system of open-source software for microfinance. Since 2005, he has continued to work with small technology firms, helping with data analysis, product definition, and R&D. A self-funded sabbatical during 2011 made possible the writing of *Giving Back*, his first book.

The material for *Giving Back* comes from Dr. Ketchpel's experience in working with and volunteering for nonprofit organizations. His first volunteer experiences were part of his years growing up in Connecticut, where he was active in Boy Scouts and the Order of the Arrow (a Scouting service organization), as well as in a Congregationalist UCC church. Applying the entrepreneurial insights of leverage and scale led him to focus on empowering others, and conversations with supporters of United Campus Christian Ministry @ Stanford (where Dr. Ketchpel was a director and fund-development committee chair) showed the impact that giving back has in people's understanding of meaning in their lives. The inspiration for *Giving Back* is to encourage more people to find and pursue the passions that simultaneously enhance life's meaning, strengthen family bonds, and make the world a better place.

Dr. Ketchpel lives in the San Francisco Bay Area.

Engage in *Giving Back*!

Visit the website http://www.giving-back.info/ to:

❖ Download blank copies of the exercises.

❖ Read and discuss the latest blog entries.

❖ Learn more about interpreting IRS 990 forms.

❖ Find links to organizations listed in the book (and others added since the book was printed).

Contact the author (ketchpel@giving-back.info) to:

❖ Share your stories of how giving back (or *Giving Back*, the book) has affected you.

❖ Propose topics for blog entries or future editions of *Giving Back*.

❖ Inquire about scheduling talks or workshops about *Giving Back*.

❖ Request review copies or inquire about discounts for nonprofits.

Follow the author on Twitter (@GivingBackBook).

❖ Propose projects and resources for him to re-tweet.

Join the community at Facebook (givingbackinfo) to:

❖ Participate in an online discussion.

❖ Find other people committed to giving back.

❖ Share events and resources.

Order copies of *Giving Back* for your friends and colleagues at:
giving-back.info/buy

14654103R10094

Made in the USA
San Bernardino, CA
01 September 2014